I've Found the Keys, Now Where's the Car?

*A journey of a thousand miles
begins with one step.*

LAO TZU

I've Found the Keys, Now Where's the Car?

Vicki Bennett

Hodder & Stoughton

A Hodder & Stoughton book

First published in Australia and New Zealand in 1996 by
Hodder Headline Australia Pty Limited
(A member of the Hodder Headline Group)
10–16 South Street, Rydalmere NSW 2116

Reprinted 1996, 1997

National Library of Australia Cataloguing-in-Publication data

Bennett, Vicki.
"I've found the keys, now where's the car?"

Bibliography.
Includes index.
ISBN 0 7336 0269 X

1. Self actualisation (Psychology). 2. Success. 3. Self-esteem.
4. Success in business. I. Title

158.1

Designed by Vivien Valk
Printed in Australia by McPherson's Printing Group

To Tammie, Cassie, Rosalind, Ellie,
Michael and Ian
the family from Heaven

Contents

Introduction

Recently, on a trip to Melbourne, I arranged to meet my Uncle Doug and Aunty Audrey. We met in the lobby of the hotel I was staying at. It was very exciting to see them looking so well and happy and to catch up with them and all the gossip about our relatives.

When it came time to go, Uncle Doug couldn't find the keys to his car. Frantically we retraced our steps, looking under tables where we had been sitting, behind chairs and under cushions. Eventually we found the keys and Doug walked off happily to locate the car. Audrey and I sat in the lobby of the hotel and waited for him to drive up the ramp to collect her for the journey home, and waited and waited. We went on talking together about her childhood, her loves, her early life and didn't notice the time passing. When we looked up, we saw a very cross and frustrated Uncle Doug hurtling up the ramp and into the reception roundabout.

'Do you realise how long I've been? Do you realise how many levels there are down there? Do you realise how they all look the same? Do you understand how hopeless these carparks are?'

We could see it all on his face, the frustration, the embarrassment, the humiliation, the feeling of not being in control. Then it dawned on me, finding the keys was only the first step, and we often think it is the only step. But in this case, finding the vehicle was the hardest step of all.

We have the *key* to our lives all the time, but many of us have forgotten where the car is parked. The *key* is your heart, the ability to open it up and express it; the car is your mind, the vehicle to show your heart to the world.

This book has been written as a guide for using all our resources: our hearts, our minds, intellects and creativity, our souls and our spirits. There are many choices available for accessing these resources and in this book you will find many *keys* to unlock your potential in all these areas. What you decide to do with your vehicle when you unlock the door is completely up to you.

As a speaker, a trainer and a management consultant, I have worked with thousands of wonderful people all over the world. Mostly I've found that they have the *key*, but need a catalyst to help them to see how they can apply it. I believe that this book will give you this catalyst, or vehicle for change.

Over the duration of the average working life it is expected that we will change our workstyle, our attitude, our behaviour at least seven times, and yet, collectively, change is our largest fear. In the book of lists, change registers higher in fear than dogs, dying and speaking in front of a crowd.

Responding to change is like playing a game of monopoly. You have to throw the dice to stay in the game. You have to take risks to play. Otherwise, you will end up growing old on Pall Mall.

As a risk taker, I believe I bring a depth of understanding, skill and knowledge to you through my experience in working with people in companies, helping them and their teams to become more productive through the acceptance of change as a constant and through becoming change proactive rather than change reactive. This book is taken from my experience in the marketplace and will empower you to realise your personal and business potential. Higher personal productivity and clearer focus are just two of the by-products of this knowledge, once applied.

I began as a salesperson at the age of eighteen. Before I had turned 20, I was promoted to the task of national and international sales trainer for the Receptionist Centre, responsible for the training and motivation of personnel in Australia and overseas. I've been in the training business ever since.

I have my own business, Vicki Bennett Training, which specialises in the attitudinal and skills training of people in corporations and companies. This has been operating successfully since 1980. I focus on effective communication, customer service skills and team building; I contribute to increasing the productivity of teams and the empowerment of the individual, through the thousands of seminars and workshops I have conducted throughout Australia and overseas. I am also called upon as a keynote speaker at many national and international conferences and conventions.

One of my passions for the past 11 years has been helping young people to learn practical business skills, through my role as Queensland chairman and a national trustee of Young Achievement Australia.

I have successfully authored three books (*Program to Succeed*, *Take Me To My Garden Mummy* and *Mirrors – An Adventure into Ourselves*). I believe that all the great achievement in business, the community and in history has come about because one person, with an idea, has been able to inspire and enthuse others. I believe we all have the potential to be that one person.

My family has been a constant source of enthusiasm for me – my husband Ian Mathieson, my parents Vida and George McGregor and our five children. They have supported me with friendship, challenges, learning, frustration, joy, fury and lots of love, and I am wiser and of greater worth for having them all in my life.

In *I've Found the Keys, Now Where's the Car?* you will find I have posed many ideas, many practised solutions, and thrown in a few challenges too, through real life stories, experiences and insights.

This book can be read in one sitting or can be flicked open and read in small portions. It can be used as a text to increase productivity within your organisation, or can be used as an effective communications manual for a partnership or marriage. It can be used as a reference for effective relationships for teenagers and adults alike. When the words resonate within your heart and mind, then you will know how to apply the knowledge.

About Elizabeth

In 1962 a small child was sitting in a large tree. She had climbed there in the late afternoon, with the raw summer sun setting, as she had every day after school for the last year. She always went as far up as she would dare. She yearned for the courage to sit right up in the fork of the tree so that she could see the most glorious of sunsets, but lacked the will to do it.

It took months, which seems a lifetime for a child of 10, but finally she reached the highest fork, and as she sat watching the sun set, a mysterious, magical feeling settled upon her. She felt the sun in her heart, she felt the tree in her limbs as if the tree were she.

She remembered who she was, she felt her heart, she felt love for every-thing around her, as if for the first time. It was like in a dream. The lights came on in her conscious mind and she struggled to keep the thought, the insight, but she knew that it was fading already.

She knew that what she had felt was important, sitting there in that tree, because she remembered, as if from somewhere else. She felt the power, the strength and the euphoric oneness with everything around her and she remembered how much she could feel love. Love of the sunset; of the beauti-ful cypress tree; of the air that felt strangely soft in the hot afternoon; of the tiny ants crawling up the tree in frenzied silence; of the leaves silently brush-ing her face as the afternoon breeze rustled in the anticipation of an early evening storm. She felt nature as if she were nature; nature and herself were everything she could feel.

This curly-headed sweet child, whom I call Elizabeth in this book, forgot that day as she grew into adolescence, womanhood, then motherhood, but it existed inside her, silently, and I now want to share her triumphs, her sadness, her achievements and her failures with you.

Elizabeth introduces each chapter of the book with a story about her life and how she learnt the lessons of life through the keys in this book. In telling her stories at the beginning of each chapter, I hope to illustrate that the key is your heart, and if you have the courage to open your heart, as she does, you will learn, by both successes and failures.

As she has done in this book, you may choose to take the risk to expose this most vulnerable part of yourself – your heart. The vehicle is your mind, and in the vehicle portions of this book you will be shown how you can use your mind effectively to express what you feel in your heart.

THE **1** KEY

Optimism

---

*'If You Think You Can,
You Can'*

THE VEHICLE

Becoming an Optimist

Elizabeth's story

Elizabeth was not born happy. As a little girl she was always crying and it was not in her nature to do things the conventional way. She was always playing too hard, or roughly, or for too long and it was a real challenge for her mother to balance her reprimands with love. Elizabeth seemed to be a person who was always in trouble.

Her mother never gave up, always commenting on the things she did that were helpful, and making a fuss over everything Elizabeth brought home from school, whether it was a soggy Anzac biscuit, a stick-people painting, or an essay with more red circles of correction on it than there was black pencil.

She was Elizabeth's greatest supporter, counsellor, coach and friend, as well as a loving mother. Elizabeth, like most children, took all this love for granted, but on the day her father came into her room, ashen-faced and hands trembling, with the horrific news of her mother's fatal car accident, she knew that her life, her love, her everything had changed from that moment.

In that instant, Elizabeth became a different person, she changed from an irritable, undesirable child to a loving, helpful girl. It was as if she had absorbed by osmosis everything her mother had taught her; everything she had seen her mother do was permanently engraved on her psyche. And there she was, this lovely child, encompassing all the loveliness of her mother, as if by pure magic.

She was always there for the younger children, always there for her Dad, listening to his stories about his hard day at the office, just like her Mum had done. But the lovely thing that she did for her sisters and brothers was to see the good in them at all times – always bringing it out, always reinforcing it, and helping them to remember it and honour it, too.

She found herself teaching them about optimism, about positive attitude, all the wondrous things she rejected as a child herself, and she felt she had the right to do this, as she had come so far to learn them. Whenever any of her sisters or brothers left the house she would say, 'You look marvellous, perfect, except for one thing, remember to take your smile.'

Whenever she said this, she could hear her mother and was reminded of the gift of optimism given to her freely and unconditionally by her Mum, and she understood that for a gift to be of value, it needs to be passed on freely and often. So she made a commitment to optimism there and then: whenever she could, she would choose the optimistic viewpoint, the optimistic attitude, the optimistic road, which is often less travelled.

Elizabeth's story

If you think you can,
you can.
If you think you can't,
you're right.

HENRY FORD

Becoming An Optimist

Every day is a new beginning. Every day, as you stumble into wakefulness, you're faced with new decisions, new dimensions, new choices. Each and every morning, you choose what sort of an attitude you will have. You make that decision when you open your eyes. Do you choose a terrific day, a day where you can achieve and find pleasure in achievement, or do you choose stress, negativity and low-level drama?

Do you look forward to what you have planned for the day? Do you decide that today is going to be your day to really excel, to turn the world upside down, or does the prospect of another ordinary day just leave you empty?

If you don't wake up feeling good about the day, that will impact on the result of your day, because the way you feel at the beginning determines what sort of day you're going to have.

Your positive mental attitude contributes 80 per cent to the success of your day, which in turn becomes your life. As Henry Ford senior once said, 'If you think you can, you can. If you think you can't, you're right.' Your thought processes, what you are thinking right now, will determine how you will see the world around you. It's your choice.

You become what you
think about.

CASSANDRA BENNETT

Create new beginnings

~~~~~~

Sally, who was a participant in a customer service workshop, told me of her experience. She worked in the service station business as a console operator and was naturally a happy, easy-going, bright soul. She enjoyed her work, as the combination of looking after customers, balancing her console and the responsibility of the job suited her well.

She served all types of people. The pensioner who bought his 'smokes' for the week every pension day. The drunks who came in at 10.00 pm wanting pies and peas, to soak up the excess fluid in their bodies. The busy business people with their mobile phones permanently pressed to their ears. The kids who would smile ear-to-ear as they held their sticky fingers out for change. She served them all with a warmth and sweetness that came from her heart.

Sally enjoyed her work until Mr Barry, a regular account customer, came into her life. He was pushy, rude and arrogant, in short the 'customer from hell'. No matter what she did, she could not get him to respond to her in a positive manner. In fact, he treated her as if she didn't exist. Over and over again, she smiled and talked to him and tried to get him to look at her, just to notice that the person serving him was also a human being, and over and over again, he treated her with arrogant indifference.

One day she decided to make an even bigger effort; he wasn't going to break her good spirits. All of a sudden he looked up, noticed her and said, '...don't be such a smart bitch'. He turned his back and left.

Sally was devastated and overcome with grief and anger that someone had spoken to her that way. She said to me, 'How can I deal with that? How do I handle that person?'

I said, 'You can't; you can't change him. He is determined to see the world his way. However, be very pleased you don't live inside Mr Barry's head, Sally, because what he is expressing is only a small part of his attitude to himself as well as to the rest of the world and it's awful.'

Sally's attitude was to notice the things that went right. His attitude was not to notice. This appeared extraordinary to Sally, as she mostly found people treated her well and that the world was mostly a happy place. Mr Barry's world was very destructive, and incredibly limiting for him and his success in life, as well as for the people around him.

So it's not so much the actual physical conditions that count in life, but the way they are handled, your mental attitude to life.

Is your glass half empty or half full?

As the sun is rising in a morning blaze, do you see the dirty window pane, or the beautiful sunrise outside the window? Is your glass half empty or half full? Is your day going to be fulfilling or hard going?

I was talking with a client called Bill recently, and he was going to great lengths describing what a stressful day he was going to have. He had it all worked out: he had a couple of meetings lined up that he was absolutely dreading; and he had grave doubts about how his people would react to our training sessions. He was literally willing the day to turn out badly, but he couldn't see that.

I started talking about how much we were going to achieve and how productive and effective the training sessions would be and just how much I was looking forward to our working together.

Stress is a choice.

DONNA DALZELL

You choose your reactions

In response, Bill looked at me in a kind of startled way and said, 'We are talking about the same day, aren't we?' He thought for a second and said, 'You know, it wouldn't be too difficult for me to change my mind about today; I'm starting to feel better about it already.' And then he went on to say, 'I will have a great day. It is my choice, isn't it?'

What do you say to your partner first thing in the morning – your wife, your husband or your lover? What do you talk about in the first few minutes of the day? Think about what you say to that person, because whatever it is you say shows the kind of relationship you have going for you.

Those first few unguarded minutes are a real giveaway. Do you jump out of bed and race out to greet the day, or do you lie there and nudge the person beside you and say, 'Come on, your turn to make the tea!'?

One of our favoured family stories is about my children's father, Duncan Bennett. He is one of life's 'jumpers'. He is a real enthusiast, and he has succeeded in passing it on to our children, Tammie and Cassie. When they were little, he worked out a little morning ritual to get them enthusiastic about the day ahead.

He'd go out in the hallway with them every morning and he'd say 'What does T-E-R-R-I-F-I-C spell?', and the girls would answer, 'Terrific'.

Our older girl, Tammie, was learning to spell and feeling quite clever about it. He found her in the hallway one morning saying to Cassie, 'What sort of a day are you going to have?', and Cassie answered, 'Terrific', and then Tammie said, 'What does C-A-S-S-I-E spell?', and Cassie answered, 'Terrific'.

You see, everything spells terrific to that little girl at that time of the morning, because that's the way she feels at that time of the morning. She's programmed to feel terrific.

This is positive programming. All too often, parents are too eager to point out the negatives: 'Don't do this... Don't forget to do that... Don't be late home... Don't forget your homework'. Interesting statements, because the subconscious mind cannot hear 'don't', so the child is really hearing: 'Forget to come home early' and 'Forget your homework'. Parents need to use active, not reactive, statements. 'Please do this... Remember to do this... Please be home at 4.00 pm.'

Children need positives from adults

Children need these positives from adults, as they impact enormously on their life; they affect their expectation of the day. Children need leadership from the 'grown ups' of the world, even though the 'grown ups' are often challenged enough attempting to program a splendid day for themselves.

Children need to learn from their poor choices or mistakes. If they are allowed to feel the disappointment or hurt of something that has gone wrong, then they are more likely to self-correct next time. Sometimes life is difficult, but if the parent tries to save the child from experiencing this, the natural consequence is that they grow up with an unrealistic view of the world. They have to learn to be responsible at some stage; a loving parent will create an environment in which this can occur by allowing the child to experience their mistakes when they happen.

At the same time, a loving parent will notice and support their child when they are getting things nearly right. Catch your children doing things right with the same vigour that the negative parent expresses when they do things wrong. These steps will have an enormously positive effect on your child and their ability to create optimism in life.

Someone who really knew from an early age how to program a splendid day for herself is Jeanne Louise Calment. She was born in Arles, in southern France, in 1875. She is the oldest human alive whose age can be authenticated. Jeanne remembers meeting Vincent van Gogh in 1888, using horse-drawn carriages and vividly recalls the era of Queen Victoria.

She is the darling of the French press with her terse comments. Asked how she has lived so long, she answers, 'God must have forgotten me', or how she views her future, 'Short'. At 100 years of age she was still riding her bicycle, and remains very fond of a glass of port served with chocolates.

But her real beauty is her attitude. The director of her nursing home says, 'She never feels sorry for herself. She has no illusions.' She did make one concession to her passing years: at age 118 she gave up smoking.

Jeanne Louise Calment understands the true meaning of being an optimist. She has always kept her eye out for the pessimists and handled them with humour and goodwill.

You become what you think about

You have to keep an eye out for the negative people and guard against their influence over you. Like Jeanne, you are responsible for what goes into your mind, and you must guard the gates to your mind. If you constantly allow negative thoughts into your mind, that's precisely what comes out again in your words and your actions. If you have ever used a computer, you would be familiar with the letters GIGO: garbage in, garbage out. Whatever is programmed into the computer is what comes out. You can't blame the hard disc; it is usually the operator who has put the wrong command or the incorrect information into it in the first place.

In order to change your life outside,
you must change inside.

LOUISE L. HAY

Guard the gates to your mind

José Silva in his book *The Silva Mind Control Method* writes about a technique that can be used to guard the gates. Whenever a repetitive, negative thought (that does not serve you well) comes into your head, one that you can't convert or solve, one that just comes under the category of 'beating yourself up' – think and say the words 'cancel, cancel...' Like a computer, the mind will respond instantly and you will gain control of your thought processes again.

Some negative thoughts are useful as they give you an opportunity to think about a possible problem or danger and work it through. But a large percentage of negative thinking is not contributing to your goals and not helping you to achieve a constructive and happy life. So for those non-constructive thoughts, apply the 'cancel, cancel...' technique.

The input you feed your mind needs to be monitored regularly. You need to feed it positive reinforcement about what you are seeing and feeling, not negative acceptance.

On rising, decide to enjoy your day and discipline yourself to balance your thought processes. Look forward to all the things that you will do and enjoy, and see them in a positive light. The negative thoughts will still come, but now they will be in better perspective.

Instead of listening to the news on the radio, which is often negative, try listening to some positive motivational audio tapes, or some beautiful, inspiring music. Learn something – it is possible to learn a new language in eight months by using this time constructively. Listen to something that's going to help inspire your spirit for the day. Use the time in the morning to its best possible advantage to educate and motivate yourself. There is so much fantastic material available on cassette – make use of it. It will put you in the right frame of mind.

The very first minutes of your working day are incredibly important, too. When you first get to work, do you just walk through the door and mumble 'Hello', or do you bound through the door with a spring in your step and greet the working day with enthusiasm? Having a positive mental attitude isn't going to solve all your problems for you, but it will improve your ability to handle them.

Monitor your thinking

Many people are afraid to admit to having a problem. They go through life too timid or too scared to ask for help. They don't want to appear dumb or incompetent in front of others. Asking for help or cooperation is not an admission of failure, and if you don't ask or give help when it's needed, everyone loses.

Asking for help means that you may draw on your team, whoever that team is, at work or at home. Working together with another person or a group improves the performance of every member of the team or family.

Working as a team intensifies performance

We can all take a lesson from Clydesdales; these beautiful 'gentle giants' of the horse family are a good example of teamwork. One Clydesdale working on its own can usually pull a load of around 9000 pounds. Put two together in harness, and they'll pull a load of around 20 000 pounds – more than double the capability of a single horse. But a well-trained pair of Clydesdale horses that have worked together for a while and know each other's strengths and weaknesses are capable of shifting 28 000 pounds.

What a difference! Individually, each horse can only pull 9000 pounds, but by pulling together, their performance is more than trebled.

How much performance could you pick up by working as a team? How much more could you achieve – not just at work but in your personal life too –

if you learnt to share the load? How much could you improve by learning and putting an effort into pulling together? It is not necessary to do it all alone; optimism shared with a team is optimism intensified. Just as the Clydesdales' ability intensifies working as a team, you can intensify your ability by working as an optimistic team.

Crisis creates opportunity

Very often, it takes a real crisis to force us into pulling together. It took Adolph Hitler and World War II to bring the British people together. Many books and films have been produced about the effective teamwork of the British people during this war, of how people broke down their barriers of prejudice during this time to work for a common cause, to win the war. But as soon as the crisis had passed and the war was won, the unity and sense of purpose of the individual passed as well and everyone started pulling in their own different direction again.

Drought, famine, fire, flood – all these horrific natural disasters have a very negative effect on people at the time, but people can draw strength from a common goal and rebuild together as a team. It is a paradox that so often we only choose to use these great team-building skills in crisis. In the Chinese language, the same character is used to represent both 'crisis' and 'opportunity'. The Chinese understand that in crisis, when one person works with another, putting aside personal preferences and differences, they can work effectively as a team.

I live in a street that was completely under water in the Brisbane 1974 floods. I wasn't living in the street at the time but a neighbour of mine, Janie, showed me the pictures of her two storey house completely under water, then she showed photos of the mud throughout the house after the floods had receded. She talked of her wedding photos being lost, of her clothes being ruined, of the work that had to be done to put their life back together after such a personal disaster; but there was a twinkle in her eye as she talked about what they created as a result of that crisis, a beautiful, almost new, home. There are also a bunch of people in the street that she has a strong, bonded relationship with, a relationship that was created by a crisis. Opportunity is a choice.

Optimism is a choice

Helen Keller faced great personal crisis because of her physical disabilities. She was totally blind and could not speak; yet she went on to touch millions of people with her words through her books. She once wrote, 'Sometimes we look at the door that's just closed in our faces so long, we fail to see the door opening just up the road a little.'

Every day brings new crises and with it new opportunities; it's unusual to have one without the other. But by developing a positive mental attitude, you'll be able to recognise the opportunity within each crisis, and grab it.

Recognise opportunity

The opportunities are always there, but most people just see the crisis. If you were a penniless migrant, just arrived in the country and barely able to speak the language, which would you see, crisis or opportunity? Every country is filled with such examples – people who decide to look at their options and create a window of opportunity, the glimpse of a chance. These people have an attitude of hope and of positive expectation. They don't wait for exactly the right job to come along; they look at what the market needs and take a punt with an idea or hunch, then put all their energy behind it and make it a reality.

Montserrat is just such a case, coming from a politically unstable and lethal region in South America. She lived in fear for her life and the lives of her family. They had reached the pinnacle of success in their native country. Her husband was a professional in his field of accountancy and she a successful teacher. They lived in a beautiful home, had a wonderfully supportive group of friends, their children were getting a first-class education and everything was roses, until the revolution.

Their life changed from privilege to bare survival. The army was intent on radical change and this family represented everything that they wanted to destroy. At first the impact was indirect: Montserrat's husband's job was real-located to someone else. Then, more directly, the school the children were attending was closed down and the children were ushered home by guards, who brutally threw them out onto the street. When Montserrat could not get food because she was refused coupons by the new regime, she knew that she and her family were in grave danger of their lives.

After months of fear and degradation they finally found a loophole in the emigration process and were able to migrate to Australia. They experienced the euphoria of arriving in a country with order and with so much opportunity. She tells me that the feeling was similar to that of a honeymoon – warmth, love and grand expectation.

It came as a surprise to both of them to find themselves depressed and missing their homeland, not their homeland of revolution and despair, but the homeland of their old memories. Everything was different, the language was confusing, the food was so different, even salt (an old and dear friend in all their native dishes) was viewed as the enemy in this bold new environment.

It was Montserrat who chose to change, and she took her partner along with her by sheer force and strength of passion. She said:

> OK, we have wallowed long enough in this grief for something that we crave and miss. This place doesn't exist any more, it has gone. We must leave it in our minds as a special place to visit, to think about, and we must now move on to this new adventure. This new country is offering us much opportunity and we are not taking it up. Our way of thinking is what will create a new life for us.

What brave words, what insight! Montserrat began the next day; she went to the local community centre and put up signs: 'Young, energetic woman available as cleaner'. She then went to all the local shops and did the same. It took her two days to find her first customer, and two weeks to fill all her available time. She then started employing others to work for her, instilling her principles and standards upon them as prerequisites for the job. Pretty soon she found that she needed her husband's knowledge of accounts and money to add to her business.

Montserrat has created her reality with her attitude and her ability to look for the chance, the opportunity. She now has a springboard to do anything she wants. The key was not to wallow in grief for long; she did not wallow in self pity or think longingly of the past, she did not say, 'I can't do this, I'm too important' – she just got on with it.

We are capable of this kind of success if we just learn to recognise the opportunities, if we concentrate on the positive aspects of life and put the negative aspects in perspective.

Positive attitude creates success

There are many people like Montserrat who possess a *positive mental attitude*. You won't necessarily find them on the rich and famous list or living in the most expensive suburb in the district. But you will find a special quality about them that shines strongly from their eyes and that you will be touched by, immeasurably. It's in their spirit, their core, and you will recognise them, as they will be ready to share their optimism with you eagerly.

A recent survey showed that most people in life are not motivated by money or material possessions, but are motivated by setting their own goals and single-mindedly achieving them. To do this you need a bag full of optimism and a bucket load of positive mental attitude.

The choice is up to you. No one is going to make you a success. It's you who has to do it. How are you going to treat tomorrow, and every other day in your life? As a day fraught with danger and risk and crisis? As just another day? Or as a day absolutely overflowing with opportunities?

If you think you can't, you're never going to do it. But if you think you can... you can.

Opportunity is now here

~~~

What the mind of man
can conceive and believe,
the mind of man can achieve.

NAPOLEON HILL

Creating Positive
Attitude and Optimism

☑ Create new beginnings

☑ Is your glass half empty or half full?

☑ You choose your reactions

☑ Children need positives from adults

☑ You become what you think about

☑ Guard the gates to your mind

☑ Monitor your thinking

☑ Working as a team intensifies performance

☑ Crisis creates opportunity

☑ Optimism is a choice

☑ Recognise opportunity

☑ Positive attitude creates success

☑ Opportunity is now here

Dreams Can Come True

---

*Believing without
the Evidence*

THE VEHICLE

Goal Setting and Visualisation

Elizabeth's story

As Elizabeth was growing into a young teenager she always took with her the image of her mother, the tenderness of her mother's touch, the brightness of her mother's smile, the loveliness of her mother's gentle, kind eyes and at night, when all around her was quiet, still she would think of her mother and visualise what her mother would say and do and make up little scenarios about how her mother would be if she were with her now.

Elizabeth was very skinny and tall, and in her mind she felt she was a very unattractive teenager. She was always the girl left out, the girl who was never asked to dance. So when she discovered that the means she used to recall her mother into her mind would also work as a means to establish a relationship with boys she was attracted to, she thought she had discovered something as earth-shattering as the meaning of life.

Every night before Elizabeth went to sleep she would imagine a story. It always made going to sleep for her a very positive thing. She imagined stories that had a lot of detail and intricate subplots. Colour, the way people looked, and their mannerisms were important aspects that made up the tapestry of her dreams before she went to sleep.

She always enjoyed this time, always enjoyed the story as it developed in her head, always loved the outcome, as she had complete control of it and in her life this was the only place where she had such control. She was often the beautiful princess who found herself in a lonely place in need of friendship and then she created an equally handsome prince to befriend her. But the more she daydreamed, instead of the handsome prince, she saw a young man whom she admired from school; his name was John. She would see herself in a modern-day setting at school, sitting feeling dumb, feeling inadequate, and John,

to her, the most handsome, most incredible, desirable boy at school, would come right up to her and talk to her and listen to her, and as they laughed and smiled together, he would be intent on her every word.

She would see them walk hand-in-hand out of the classroom, barely remembering where they were and pulling their hands apart just in time as the teacher turned the corner, seeing them only with a happy look on their faces. Elizabeth saw herself and John arriving together at the school dance, looking wonderful, feeling wonderful; all eyes were upon them, envying them, and everyone wished they were in her shoes.

She found to her absolute amazement that not long after she had been dreaming these things, they began to happen. Elizabeth laughed to herself when the smartest, bravest, most desirable boy at school, John, asked her out and began to write love poems to her. It was all so hard to believe, these things didn't happen to ugly ducklings. But she looked in the mirror again and again and, faintly, she began to see a more beautiful person looking back at her.

'No,' she thought to herself, she couldn't have transformed herself into something as beautiful as she had seen in her dreams. It couldn't be true. And yet it was happening. And she started to believe it.

Elizabeth started to dream up all sorts of things: improving her scholastic results, achieving better swimming times, improving her relationship with her father, but mainly her relationships with boys. Where most of her friends were living the lives of their parents' design, Elizabeth was majoring in dreaming her dreams and reaping the benefits of a beautiful romance and a positive life. The paradox of it all was how this ability had come out of the most terrible crisis, the death of her mother.

Elizabeth's story

Man is made by his beliefs.
As he believes, so he is.

BHAGAUAO-GITA

Goal Setting and Visualisation

Every year, the world's coastlines and estuaries provide wintering grounds for countless millions of migrating birds. They arrive at the same spot year after year after year, even young birds who have never made the trip before.

How do they do it? How do they find their way half way around the world to a destination they've never seen before?

Research suggests that the birds possess a genetic coding that enables them to do this. They know precisely where they're going, even before they leave their nesting grounds. They know because in effect they're born with a memory of the future. As with the migrating birds, you can memorise where you want to go and what you have to do to get there.

The subconscious can be programmed to act as your autopilot in life. In great detail, feed in all the information needed for a smooth flight. Your final destination. Course adjustments. Height. Speed. Every last detail up to and including the final touchdown.

Develop your future memory

You need to develop your future memory, too. You need to have arrived at your chosen destination even before you start on your journey through life. It's about setting goals, and achieving them by using visualisation.

David and Angelo were great mates; they shared a common love of classical music, their families, and of fine wines. They were neighbours in Queensland's Granite Belt winemaking district and they shared many sunsets together sitting on the back verandah of David's property sharing a bottle of wine, usually one that Angelo, a professional winemaker, had made.

The sunsets were breathtaking, the reds and yellows interweaving as lovers do to make the most perfect finalé, and the coolness and freshness of the air cleansing the surrounding grapevines as they gently grew into the most succulent of fruits for making into the most fragrant and pallet-cleansing wines. It was during one of these superb sunsets that the germination of an idea, the creation of an event, was first spoken of.

David and Angelo had a future memory which became a vision, a vision to share their love of classical music, their love of the district, their love of the wines of the district, and the love of this beautiful sunset. They created an idea to stage 'Opera at Sunset' and they would bring hundreds of people from all over the place to share these special attractions.

They did not make this decision with their heads, they made it with their hearts and cemented it with their spirits; and they set about making it a reality by inspiring firstly their wives Del and Mary, their families, their friends, then their whole community with their vision. They made it come true.

David didn't make it to the first 'Opera at Sunset'; he died shortly before his dream came true. But his spirit is in the setting of the sun, in the rustling of the trees and in the sound of the clear beautiful voices of the performers. He, his life partner Del and their friends Angelo and Mary took that dream by using their future memory and created a goal that the world can now share.

Jenny was an artist, a passionate creator of ideas onto canvas; her passion was visible in her eyes when she spoke of her latest painting, in her breath as she explained her creation, and in her gaze as she lovingly studied her work. Jenny married later in life rather than earlier and transferred her love of art into love for her husband.

All went well for Jenny in her life until one day she woke up and realised that the demands of her partner, James, were overriding her personal need to paint. She told him about her need to follow her passion and set about rekindling her skills and love of painting. She was thwarted at every turn, not by James directly telling her not to paint but by the constant demands he made on her, which, with her lovely nature, she could not refuse.

Eventually she realised if she did not set goals for herself, her work, her relationship and her life, she would never be able to paint again. Although she was constantly getting opposition from James, she still had goals and aspirations in all areas of her life and because she had these planned out and had them firmly visualised in her imagination she achieved the balance she desired.

Last time I saw her she had just won the major art prize from her district, and she was very happy in life and love.

The most important thing about goals is having one.

GEOFFRY F. ABERT

Lorraine was finding life in her 80s very difficult. Her loving family was constantly fretting about her, fussing about everything she did. The next step, she knew, was for them to make her a resident in the local aged home and while many of her friends were living in the centre, she wanted the freedom of looking after herself.

Lorraine had a passion. For 10 years she had collected every piece of information she could about the Information Superhighway. She came from the era that had borne the children who had, in turn, borne the children who now surfed on this Superhighway. Despite her age, she was totally and absolutely fascinated about how it was done and how the technology could give so much freedom to people to communicate with each other.

Three earth-shattering things happened at once on Lorraine's 87th birthday. Her children sold her home, they made her a resident in the district aged home, and her grandson Tony gave her a computer system and a modem and hooked her up to the Internet. Lorraine was in fear, everything she knew was changed, everything she trusted and understood was in disarray.

After feeling absolute despair and depression for several months, she suddenly realised that life had indeed passed her some lemons but she was an old trouper and had been through more change in her lifetime than most people had had hot breakfasts; she was not going to let this massive upheaval beat her. She was going to set some goals, she was going to make a difference. Why not? Goal setting had always worked for her in the past. So, with renewed courage and vigour, she set her goals and set out to achieve them.

Her goals were not to be taken lightly, even though the staff and the residents of her home were not very supportive of her, saying she was too old, too inexperienced, too uneducated. The goals Lorraine has achieved to date include learning the keyboard, mastering her computer, and surfing the Internet, including learning backgammon from an avid player in Russia who took the time through the Internet to show her how to play and, she suspects, even let her win once or twice to boost her self confidence. Her new goals include setting up a newsletter on the Internet for senior citizens in her district, teaching three people a month to surf the Internet, and to play backgammon with a person from every country in the world within 10 years.

When Lorraine goes to sleep at night she doesn't have to remember to visualise her goals. She floats off to sleep with visions of Nova Scotia, Berlin, India – of accessing these countries through a communication system that she had the courage to learn.

Both Jenny and Lorraine successfully used goal setting and visualisation to create their future memory; their goals became their target, and their visualisation the autopilot to achieve these goals.

To create the environment to set goals we sometimes need a hint, an idea of where we need to go, so remembering past journeys and successes is a way of creating future success and achievements. So before creating the future, remind yourself of your peak experiences from the past, the time or times in your life when you have felt 'in charge' and in control of your destiny. Set the scene in your conscious and subconscious mind for future success by using this exercise, to recreate the positive feelings of the past.

Recalling a peak experience exercise

Allow yourself a few moments to recall one of your own peak experiences. Think back over your personal bests – occasions when, for some reason, you were better than you usually are. Select one that you can recall quite clearly. It may have been at work, while under pressure to perform, or with the family, or even when you were involved with your favourite sport or recreation.

A young man or woman may recall the experience where he or she was able to go to the aid of someone injured on the playing fields. A woman may recall that, in the middle of her own grief at losing her sister in a fatal car accident, she was able to come out of her fog of despair and help her sister's daughter to deal with the loss of her mother. A business person may recall a time when all the preparation, thought and time put into the planning of a proposal for business growth was rewarded by the group deciding to go ahead with the plan, taking the company into the next decade and era of growth and development. A child may remember the day at school when they first met their best friend, the one that always sticks up for them, no matter what.

Give yourself 60 seconds at this point to close your eyes and recall an experience where you really impressed yourself, as vividly as you can. You are targeting the experience itself, rather than its outcome.

Cast your mind back to that moment and recall what you were doing, how you were feeling, your posture, your emotions, your physical feelings, your level of motivation, your behaviour, the expression on your face and the faces around you. Try to recreate the moment in your mind as if it were happening now. When you have experienced that reflection long enough to recall the situation as if it were actually happening, open your eyes.

Now you have confirmed a number of things. You are capable of functioning at a level higher than your normal level of effectiveness. Since you can recall it, you know that you have the capacity within you to create it again; so if it has happened once, it can happen again. This creates an understanding. You have a peak effectiveness that, clearly, you are capable of reaching. All that remains now is to determine the process to repeat it.

Visualise future success

~~~~

When you visualise future success and think about your past triumphs, your subconscious will begin to treat all of it as if it were real. When you do this, the future will become as real, as solid, as believable as your past. As far as your mind is concerned, the future will have already happened and when you believe in something that strongly, when you can see it and taste it and hear it, then there's no way in the world it won't happen.

It's like planning for your annual holidays, the two or three weeks of the year when you know exactly where you're going and what you're going to be doing. Do you go to great lengths to plan your once-yearly getaway? How much money you need? What clothes to take? Where you will be on any given day? The planning can start weeks, months before when you put in your application for leave. It's not just a matter of waking up one morning and saying, 'Hey, I feel like a holiday. Let's go to Tasmania.' You usually plan your holidays. The time's too important just to let it slip by.

Well, what about the rest of the year? Isn't that time important, too? Why is it sometimes wasted? Plan your whole life. Find a quiet place with a pen and a goal sheet and commit yourself, concentrate on where you're going. What do you want to do with the rest of your life? Where and who do you want to be in the future?

Start moving in a positive direction

~~~~

The secret is actually sitting down, taking the time and writing down your goals. Probably the hardest part of goal setting is working out what your goals are in the first place. Students of all ages will often say, 'If I don't know what I want, how can I ever hope to achieve it?' Good point. If you don't have a direction or a target, how do you know what to aim for? Getting started is essential. If you don't make a goal or set a direction, you may find yourself feeling frustrated and helpless. If you don't have a specific goal, then start with whatever you can think of. Sometimes it seems easier not to start because you are waiting for the perfect goal or direction. There isn't one. You just have to get going.

If getting started is your particular problem, decide that by the end of this month, by a certain date, you will know what your primary goal in life will be. Then write it down, otherwise you'll just keep putting it off. Procrastination is the thief of time. If you keep putting decisions off until tomorrow, you'll eventually run out of tomorrows. Make the decision now. Today.

A child will sometimes tell you, 'When I get out of school and go to work, then I'll be happy.' A teenager will say, 'When I get a job/go to university, I'll be happy.' Then it's, 'When I find my life partner and have a family, I'll be happy.' The forty-something parents then say, 'When the kids are married and settled with their own families, then I'll be happy.' Later it becomes: 'I retire in a few years, won't things be just wonderful?' And then, when they are on their way to their funeral, they say, 'Oh no, I forgot to be happy.' Programming this sort of negative goal setting works against what you really desire.

Go for setting goals and making plans, but live in the present. Say things to yourself like, 'I really enjoy learning, and I'm going to make school fun,' and 'I am enjoying university/my first job,' and 'I'm here now in this relationship, so I had better make the most of this experience, as I may never have another one like it.'

Life can be so much easier and happier if you're working towards a clearly defined goal. It may be true to say, 'I don't care what happens to me, I can handle anything that might come my way.' But why wait for a crisis, why wait till things start going wrong before you start acting? In making positive decisions and setting active goals for yourself, there will be far fewer crises for you to handle.

Goal setting is about the future, but enables you to live for today

Goal setting is about the future, but it enables you to live for today. If you don't know where you're going, it's hard to monitor whether you are getting there or not. And whether we admit it or not, we are constantly looking for ways of monitoring ourselves. Take small steps to achieve your goal every day.

Bruce, who was several kilos overweight and very unfit, had a goal of becoming fit and healthy and had the ideal weight clearly defined in his head, but he just couldn't get started.

His goal was clear, his visualisation was crystal clear, but his flesh was unwilling. He broke the cycle of obesity by setting realistic small goals every day and monitoring himself daily to see whether his behaviour matched that goal. He gave himself three choices of exercise every day: first choice half an hour's brisk walk, second choice 20 minutes on the stationary bicycle, or third choice 30 minutes swimming.

These were attainable daily steps for him to follow to achieve his dream, and they were measurable, so that every day he could check his short-term commitment against his long-range goal. Bruce took six months to achieve his ideal weight and his desired fitness level, but could not have got started without taking these small steps and having enormous faith that the outcome would occur.

Taking small steps daily and comparing your behaviour with your goal is an extremely effective way of monitoring your progress. Don't get sucked into the negativity of comparing yourself with others. Comparing yourself with someone else is never very satisfying, because you usually compare yourself with someone who shares little in common with you.

How can you compare an apple with an orange? Both are very flavoursome, both satisfy hunger, both satisfy a need at the time, but the basics are completely different. So comparing yourself against another human being is not comparing 'apples with apples' and is not a very satisfactory or relevant measure. The only true comparison is to compare yourself with where you want to be at any given time.

So success is setting out to achieve a goal, big or small, earth-shattering or not, and taking small steps to achieve it every day.

Break your own barriers

Look at any successful sportsperson. They all set themselves goals. Every day they try to beat their personal best, breaking their own barriers. They concentrate on a specific goal. They see themselves breaking their record, right down to the actual time and distance. A sportsperson can spend anything from five minutes to five hours a day concentrating on achieving that goal. They'll visualise themselves achieving that goal. They rehearse every move in their head before they go out into the field.

Just as sportspeople use goal setting and visualisation techniques to produce results, so do young people looking to improve their personal best. I've watched young men and women of 16 and 17 years use the Young Achievement program to achieve their goals and objectives.

Kylie was in her second last year of high school when she joined the Young Achievement program. Young Achievement Australia is a program in which young people in their second last year at high school can build and become part of a business for a period of that year. Thirty students from two to four different schools are placed together with a sponsor company to choose a board of directors, decide on a product or service, sell shares to raise capital to get started and, with the help of advisers from the sponsor company, build a viable business over this six month period. At the end of this year they liquidate the company and return a profit (almost always) to their shareholders.

Before leaving the safety of school, Kylie wanted the experience of running a business, with the support of advisers who could help her, so she was very keen to be an active member of her Young Achievement group. She was very unsure of herself, but knew this much – being accepted into the program was an opportunity, and she was going to learn as much as she could from it.

In the first meeting, 25 motley-looking students from three different local high schools arrived at the sponsor company's doorstep ready for action. One of their first tasks was to appoint a board of directors to lead the group. Kylie was not a natural leader; the most she had ever led was the line to the tuckshop at school. With enormous daring, however, she put up her hand for managing director.

She had one week to come up with a speech, which would convince her peers that she should be chosen as the best person for the job. She thought of nothing else. She read the Young Achievement manual 20 times. She looked inside herself and asked if she really had the commitment that would make her the best person for the job. She looked at the picture from the other side, the side of her peers, those people whom she would be leading through the process of choosing a product to make, researching and developing the product, raising capital by selling shares, creating a production division, a selling team, an accounting team and much, much more. Could she do it? Could she be a strong, helpful leader, and could she give so much of her time to an activity outside schoolwork?

Kylie was willing to do all these things and when she spoke at the meeting for the election of board members, the others could see and feel her commitment in her language and hear it in her soft, clear voice.

Kylie was chosen managing director of the company Y.A. Creations. She made decisions, set goals, dealt with the challenge of running a business with 25 young, exuberant friends, and the occasional wild card. She chose to break her own barriers. On the surface she was the girl at school least likely to achieve and teachers and students alike were very surprised to hear that Kylie was chosen to lead the Young Achievement team.

At the end of her term as managing director she chose to enter the Young

Achievement Student of the Year competition. She didn't get into the finals, but she broke her own barriers to enter the competition and experienced success simply by 'having a go'.

Mark was working in a firm of accountants. He enjoyed the people but after 20 years in the one job found the work a little repetitive and that it wasn't extending his abilities. Mark had a secret passion: he loved model trains. He had the most elaborate and intricate layout under his house, and every night he couldn't wait to get home to tinker with his first love.

Mark felt trapped and unhappy until he broke his own barrier, left his job and, with a small loan from the bank, set up his own hobby shop, specialising in model trains. No one was going to give him that happiness except himself, and in following his passion, he created his success for himself.

Create eternity

Arthur Stace was a driven man, and his goal, his success, was to spread the message of 'Eternity' to the people of Sydney. Every weekend for 37 years, between 1930 and 1967, Arthur would take his bag of sandwiches, put on his hat and coat and stride out to write one word, the same word, 'Eternity', in yellow chalk, on as many pavements as he could before night's end.

He started early, usually before dawn, and was delighted when train lines were built to the outlying suburbs, as he was able to spread his word further than ever before. For decades this divine prank mystified the city.

Madman? Who can judge? A man on a mission? Yes, most definitely, and a man who was succeeding. He set out to write 'Eternity' on as many pavements as he could in his lifetime, to share his vision of the future.

Perhaps Arthur even achieved eternity himself. Apart from writing his word 500 000 times in his lifetime and arousing the curiosity of who knows how many people, he achieved his eternity here on earth. He is immortalised in a comic song and his story was taken up by Remo, the retailing group, and was splattered across the skyline of Sydney in a promotion of Remo and of the

33

spirit of 'Eternity'. Artist Martin Sharp vividly remembered his first brush with 'Eternity' and, like many others, continues to be captivated by the 'Eternity' enigma. Martin, in conjunction with Remo, created a small number of limited prints with the one word 'Eternity' in yellow, replicating the original chalk lines of Arthur Stace. All of this because of one man who had a goal and took small steps every day to achieve it.

You too can use small steps to achieve your goals and create the results you wish for in your life. Once you've taken the step of deciding on your main goal in life, the rest becomes a lot easier. You can then work out all the actions you need to create that goal. You can map out an *action plan*, a list of all the things that need to happen for you to achieve that goal.

Some people think that success in life is an imported car or an expensive home. These might be one of your goals, but true success is setting down a pre-determined goal about anything – relationships, family, achievement, sport, gardening, whatever – and doing everything in your power to achieve it.

Success equals goal achievement

Success is the teacher who always wanted to be a teacher, loves teaching, and is continually trying to improve his or her performance as a teacher. Success is a mother who takes pride in bringing up her children and caring for her environment, who develops and changes as her role and tasks change. Success is the businessperson who knows he or she is good at what they do and is constantly improving their performance. Success is the community worker who looks to improve living standards for others. Success is the salesperson who enjoys being a salesperson, who'd rather be a salesperson than anything else and takes pleasure in communicating with others and achieving his or her target every month.

Success is achieving what we set out to achieve. Sure, money's a part of it. Monetary success is a goal like any other, and if it's written down as a clearly defined target, it will be achieved as surely as any other goal.

As a trainer, I worked with one of Australia's leading insurance companies. The salespeople were all on commission only, and when I asked them to write down how much money they wanted to earn in the next 12 months, they were all a little bit inhibited and embarrassed.

'It's hard to say' ... 'Depends how good I am' ... 'Don't know.'

Well, after a lot of encouragement, they decided to give it a go. Sam wanted $35 000, Evonne wanted $40 000 and Betty wanted $42 500. They looked at these figures every day, and every day they were reminded of their targets. They began to visualise themselves reaching that target.

Once you have a goal, once you know where you're going, and what the end product will be, you can overcome all obstacles in the way.

Twelve months later I went back and saw these people again. I asked, 'How did you go?' Sam, who wanted $35 000, got just over that. Evonne wanted $40 000 and got $40 500. Betty, who wanted $42 500, earned $42 580. I was so happy for them, and I thought they would be too. But they seemed a little disappointed, and I was curious to know why.

Do you know what they said? 'If we'd known it was going to work, we'd have made our money targets higher.'

Money is a very understandable goal for us all, but most of the people I've worked with over the years have hopes and desires far beyond money.

Shoot for the moon. Even if you miss it,
you will land among the stars.

LES BROWN

Set clear, specific goals

So when you're writing down goals, sure, start with money, but don't let it end there. The goal setting sheets here show what I mean. There are three areas:

◆ SELF IMPROVEMENT GOALS *can include better personal health, improved education or learning, and a better style of personal living. They can include achieving a specific weight or giving up a particular personal habit.*

◆ BUSINESS/WORK, FINANCIAL AND CAREER GOALS *can include doing what you want to do, increasing financial income, determining where you want to be in five years' time, and improving your relevance in the workplace.*

◆ FAMILY AND PERSONAL GOALS *can include improving your relationship with loved ones, family or friends, finding a new home, a new car, boat or household items, buying new clothes, or that holiday you've been promising yourself for the past few years.*

You have to decide clearly what it is you want: not the things you might occasionally wish for or want in a half-hearted way, but the important things in your life. You're mapping out your life, writing down a game plan for the next five, 10, 15 years. Then write down your goals as specifically as possible. Don't be vague, list them with as much detail as possible.

Now, on the right-hand side of the page, write down the date by which you wish to achieve each goal. Be specific about it.

At the top of the page, write down the day on which you set yourself these goals. Then, as you accomplish each goal, you can cross it off your list, and you'll see just how effective this goal sheet has been.

Goal setting exercise   *Today's date: 27/05*

◆ SELF IMPROVEMENT GOALS   DATE BY

Be my perfect weight 30/10

Improve my relationship with Sue 05/06

Improve my personal attitude by
being more positive..27/06

Exercise 3 times a week..04/06

Upgrade my presentation to look fit,
healthy and well presented 27/06

Use good language in my communication...................04/06

◆ BUSINESS/WORK, FINANCIAL
AND CAREER GOALS   DATE BY

Pay out personal loan...06/11

Gain diploma in business education............................12/12

Learn the database 27/06

Get along well with Tim...30/06

Gain a salary raise..30/10

◆ FAMILY AND PERSONAL GOALS   DATE BY

Improve relationship with my partner 08/08

Go on family holiday at Christmas
with all the family...24/12

Keep my dressing area neat and organised.................05/06

Garden once a week..30/06

Build my relationship with Sonya...............................04/07

Here is an example of the action plan to follow the goal sheet.

Action plan exercise   *Today's date 27/05*
(What you are prepared to do short term to achieve the goal)

◆ **ACTION PLANS FOR**
   SELF IMPROVEMENT   **STARTING DATE**

Increase amount of fruit and vegetables,
and decrease amount of red meat 27/05
Spend half an hour a day with Sue 27/05
Check my self talk daily for 80% positive,
20% fixing mistakes 27/05
Wake up at 6.15 for morning exercise 27/05
Clean shoes weekly, throw out old underwear,
buy new stuff 30/05
Think before I speak 27/05

◆ **ACTION PLANS FOR BUSINESS/WORK,**
   FINANCIAL AND CAREER GOALS   **STARTING DATE**

Put aside $50 per week for loan 10/06
Enrol in course and pay fees 15/06
Spend 1 hour a day to learn database 27/05
Listen to Tim and support his work 15/06
Apply for salary increase 16/10

◆ **ACTION PLANS FOR FAMILY AND**
   PERSONAL GOALS   **STARTING DATE**

Spend face-to-face time with Bill every night 27/05
Book family holiday and check everyone's dates 28/06
Tidy up dressing area and throw out old clothes 29/05
Spend 1 hour gardening every Saturday/Sunday 30/06
Spend 2 hours a week talking and
listening to Sonya 27/05

Read the lists each day. Visualise yourself in the process of achieving each goal. See yourself enjoying your new income, your new car, your job, your relationships. Paint the scene vividly. Believe in it; you're developing your future memory, and after a while it will be so ingrained in your subconscious that it will be real.

The major secret to goal setting is writing the goals down in detail and putting a date for when you want to achieve them (a time frame), otherwise they'll never get past being dreams. Once you have written them down, you are well on your way to being in the top three per cent of people who feel they are in control of their lives.

The following was taken from a small business survey:

◆ **DEFINITE WRITTEN GOALS**

    3%   People felt in control and were financially wealthy

◆ **DEFINITE GOALS**

    10%   People felt they were achieving and had above average income

◆ **SOME IDEAS**

    60%   People felt they were not in control and were earning the basic wage

◆ **NO GOALS**

    27%   People felt they were victims of life and were on social security or welfare.

Develop a detailed plan of action

~~~~~~

At the same time as you set out your goals, you consciously have to develop a detailed, scheduled plan of action to bring about your goal. Every day, you have to take at least one step towards your goal. So in writing out your action plan, remember that this is a short term action, what you will do daily or weekly. Let's say if your long-term goal is to improve your relationship with your eldest son, on your goal sheet you could write, 'I will create a happy, calm environment for my son and I to have an equal relationship which is satisfying to us both.'

On the action sheet you could write: 'Spend four hours face-to-face weekly in the following areas: sport, homework and at the dinner table, interacting one-on-one with my son.'

Ensuring that goals work

◆ *Decide exactly what you want – what you strongly, sincerely and ardently desire – remember, the more emotive you become, the more likely you are to achieve that goal.*

◆ *Write down your goals in order of importance.*

◆ *Develop a detailed plan of action to achieve that goal. Take one step at a time. Do not get impatient.*

◆ *Write today's date at the top of the page.*

◆ *Then, after the goal itself, write the day you wish to accomplish your goal.*

◆ *Read your goal list first thing in the morning and last thing at night.*

◆ *Vividly imagine (see, hear, touch, smell) yourself attaining that goal.*

◆ *Expect to achieve each goal – remember, the subconscious mind cannot tell the difference between vividly imagined information and reality.*

Match your behaviour with your goal

So you have created the goal, and in the action plan you then match your behaviour to that goal. You are making it come alive on a day-to-day basis and can measure how you are going by the amount of action you are prepared to put in to achieving your goal.

If any of these goals involve other people, such as family or business partners, talk it over with them. If the goal is something you both desire, or will benefit them as well, it may result in extra support for you. Of course, there are always personal goals which you need to keep private; that's fine.

It is important to think confidently about your goals; after all, you know your goals are achievable. If you think and act confidently and successfully, you will become confident and successful. Goal setting needs you to believe without the evidence, which is a giant leap of faith.

Why not go out on a limb? That's where the fruit is.

WILL ROGERS

Watch out for the limited thinkers

It is amazing, but once you start living and thinking positively, you begin to notice the negative people in the world, the limited thinkers, the knockers. The friends who'll tell you that what you're doing is impossible. Be prepared for them, because you're going to meet a few of them. They will say things like: 'You can't do that; it will never work in this marketplace' ... 'You won't have enough money to do that' ... 'It's been done before and didn't work.' Sure, it may have been done before, but the timing may have been out; it may be that people weren't ready for it and could be ready now. Just remember, from the 'limited thinking' viewpoint what you're doing seems impossible. People can give you a hundred good reasons why it won't happen. It's almost as if they don't want it to happen. From their perspective, what you are doing is scary or intimidating.

So guard your mind. Listen to their objections, but understand they are *their* objections not yours. Don't let the seed of doubt into your mind or your life. Be prepared for negative people. It is *their* perception, not yours.

Everything and anything is possible

People often say, 'It is impossible.' If only they could open their eyes and see their situations in a new light. Everything is possible. Whatever the mind can make up or dream can be achieved. Your mind places no limitations on you, you do it to yourself. Any idea can be achieved. It is only our negative conditioning, or that of others, that stops us from following our ideas through.

Of course, it can be reasonable for others to be wary of your decisions or goals and frightened for you, but mostly they are telling you about themselves, about their own fears and anxiety. It is not really about you and your goals at all. Listen to those fears – they may be giving you some useful direction – but balance that fear against all you have to gain in achieving that goal.

Pat yourself on the back

You have to handle success as well as failure and sometimes that is even harder. Expect to achieve each and every one of your goals and, when you do, give yourself a pat on the back. 'That's great, you're terrific, you did it.' Don't just shrug your shoulders and say, 'Oh well, what's next?'

Ken, a family friend, showed me just how hard not patting yourself on the back can be, and how it can have a strong negative impact. He is a leader in the world of professional horseracing. He is a horse trainer, and every time he had any kind of success he would expand the number of horses he trained or extend the stables or buy new equipment. He never seemed to stop and acknowledge his achievement when he did have a win or major victory.

When he was nearly 50 years young, he was ready to 'chuck it in'. He had worked long hours and done well, but who cared. All of his children had left home and hardly visited him any more and he had no experience of anything outside horseracing. He barely had anything in common with his wife and partner of 30 years outside racing, and he couldn't see the point of anything. He felt burnt-out and disappointed, disappointed because he hadn't taken the time out to enjoy, to reward himself, to give himself any acknowledgment along the road.

Remarkably, he believed people are never too old or too dumb to learn, and he still has a flourishing horse-training business. He and his wife now take time out to reward themselves with all sorts of things: time with their children and grandchildren, their new and growing interest in gemstone hunting, and trips to see their long-time friends in the north. In fact, Ken says that he will reward himself with things he hasn't even thought of yet, outings and activities that bring back the sparkle to his life.

You've earned your success, let yourself enjoy it. You have to reinforce success positively. If your system has not allowed that little pat on the back, you'll short-circuit your success, and you won't feel encouraged to achieve the next goal, and the goal after that.

That's right, the next goal – your goals will be constantly updated and revised and added to, because your goals will be changing with the progression of your values and focus through life.

Change is a constant

One of the only consistent things in life is change and your goals will need to be revised to keep up with your changing situation. Many people fear success because they fear the change that they know will inevitably go with it. The human race has always shown resistance to change. If it's not uncomfortable, it's not real change. So dealing with change is a large part of the process of setting goals.

Add fire to your goals

Goals are like a fire burning fiercely. You can't say to the fire: 'First you give me heat, then I'll give you wood.' You have to build the fire, and keep adding fuel and kindling and stoking it, if you want to keep it burning brightly.

Keep adding fuel to the fire. Keep adding goals to your list. Your life will have so much more meaning if you feel you are heading in a direction of your making. It takes time. It takes energy. It can take money. But it can be such a joy to be devoting yourself to personally rewarding goals. They're yours. You're working for yourself – you are mapping out your direction.

Using both sides of the brain

We have two sides of the brain that help us achieve our goals, and we need to use both sides to make these goals a reality. The diagram below will help you to understand the basic functions of the different sides of the brain.

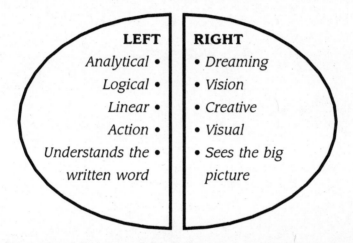

LEFT

Analytical •
Logical •
Linear •
Action •
Understands the •
written word

RIGHT

• Dreaming
• Vision
• Creative
• Visual
• Sees the big
picture

Initially, we use the right side by dreaming and creating the goals. The left brain is then activated to record the goals, then write down an action plan of what you are prepared to do to achieve the goals.

The magic occurs when you use a technique called *visualisation*, which uses the right brain function. This technique has been used for years by people who believe in the value of the subconscious mind and its power over the conscious mind. Visualisation is seeing in vivid detail your goal as it will be when you achieve it. You need to believe without the evidence that the goal will occur.

As you are going to sleep at night and as you are waking up in the morning, vividly imagine yourself as you will look, feel and be when you achieve your dream. It is really important for you to use your imagination in this exercise, as the more vividly you can imagine it, the closer you will become to making it a reality.

The subconscious mind does not know the difference between something that is vividly imagined and something that actually happens. For instance, have you ever woken up in the morning and wondered whether you have dreamt something or whether it actually happened? This is the subconscious mind working: what you vividly imagine is as real as what happens. If you vividly imagine something, the subconscious will work toward achieving it.

Use visualisation as a tool

Vince Lombardi, the famous American Gridiron coach, claimed that any successful training program needs to be 75 per cent mental and 25 per cent physical. Mental preparation wins on the day. Most teams are usually pretty well matched physically, so it's the team that has prepared themselves mentally through visualisation, the team that believes it the most on that day that wins – and you too can be mentally prepared by learning to use visualisation.

The only limitations you have are those you put there

As we relax into the subconscious level of the brain, as the mind and the body slow down and start getting ready for sleep, the limits on the mind seem to disappear. It's the best time of the day for visualisation. Spend five or 10 minutes just before you go to sleep thinking positive thoughts, visualising your goals. See yourself achieving them. It actually helps you to get a good night's sleep, because very often the visualisation will continue while you're asleep. The subconscious mind takes over and reinforces things. You'll wake up refreshed and rearing to go, and when you reinforce your goals again in the morning, it acts to remind the subconscious of what the target is.

Visualisation exercise

As you are relaxing and going toward sleep at night, imagine that you are walking up some magnificent marble stairs. Slowly, as you climb these stairs, you become more and more relaxed, more and more at peace with yourself. You reach the top of the stairs and see a door which is painted in your favourite colour. As you open the door you see a room filled with all of your friends and family who love you.

They welcome you and you sit in the middle of the room. Everyone is happy to see you and you feel wanted and welcomed and relaxed. Look around you and see that everyone is happy, and is happy to see you. Now stand up and walk toward the other side of the room and there you will find another door.

Open it and discover that behind that door is a beautiful garden full of your favourite trees, shrubs and flowers. Walk over to the biggest tree and sit beneath it. Lay back under it and look up into the sky; it is blue and beautiful and has tiny wisps of white cloud brushing over it.

You feel calm and clear and completely at ease. As you are lying there, imagine someone very close to you, someone who you trust completely, sitting beside you. Imagine that they are in complete harmony with you, understanding all your thoughts and feelings without any judgement.

Now stand up and go over to a little stream that is running through the garden. There is a big rock in the middle of the stream and you leap safely on to that rock and settle yourself on it. Now take your shoes and socks off and gently dangle your feet in the water and let them feel cool and refreshed and free. Let all your negative emotions and feelings collect in your stomach and then let them go down through your legs, through your feet and out through your toes and down the stream. You sit back and watch the ball of negative feelings flow rapidly down the stream and out into the ocean and away from you.

You feel relaxed, safe, calm and peaceful. Enjoy that feeling for a moment and then when you are ready, put your shoes and socks on and stand up from the rock and go back under the tree and sit there and imagine achieving all your goals. Enjoy the feeling of success and pride in achieving these and let yourself feel the achievement and pleasure.

See the people involved in your goal, see the surroundings. See their reactions and feel the feeling of overwhelming pride in your achievement. Then, when you are ready, take three deep breaths down into your diaphragm, and open your eyes. If it's time for sleep, just let yourself drift off to a night's sleep. Otherwise, you will feel relaxed and refreshed as a result of this exercise.

Believe without the evidence

Winston Churchill, during World War II, used visualisation several times during the day to refresh himself mentally and he believed this 10 minute process not only contributed to his success as a leader, but it enabled him to work 18 hour days and to give his best.

I know many people who use this technique in the middle or end of a busy day, not only to visualise their goals, but to refresh and regenerate their bodies. Ten minutes on this level of the brain, called the *alpha level*, gives you the feeling of the equivalent of 90 minutes of sleep, because the alpha level is the level that refreshes and calms the brain. By using the alpha level to program your goal through visualisation, the thought pattern goes directly through the alpha level to be absorbed into the subconscious.

Plant the crop and water it

In the end, we're all responsible for our own success or failure. We're responsible for planting the seed (*goal setting*) and watering the plant (*visualisation*). When a farmer plants a crop, the land doesn't care whether the farmer plants corn or weeds; it gives back whatever is planted. So make sure you plant glorious thoughts in your mind. Feed yourself positive visualisation and you'll reap a rich harvest.

Whatever you do, don't think about past mistakes and failures. The subconscious will visualise those just as enthusiastically. Think about the way you'd like to handle a situation – the way you'd like things to happen. It has an effect similar to that of a rehearsal. In your head you've already done it well once.

Geoff Richards, the Australian Rugby Union player, went to see his old mentor, John Bay, for some tactical advice when he was selected to play against France in the early 1980s. Geoff was picked as the fullback and goal kicker, but was worried about his kicking ability.

So John Bay gave him a mental exercise to do every time he lined up to kick the ball. First, he had to turn the white goal posts to red, his favourite colour. After he had placed the ball and walked back, he had to think about three big goals he'd converted in his life, all 50 yarders.

As he remembered what had happened and how good he'd felt about it, he stepped back and focused again on the goal posts and visualised a line of arrows between him and the target, like you see drawn on to newspaper photographs. He had to concentrate totally on that, forget the crowd and the other team. Geoff Richards converted the winning goal against France.

Visualisation is a skill like any other. At first it takes practice, but the more you do it, the easier it becomes. If you've mentally rehearsed an event 10 or even 20 times before it happens, you will be able to handle it better. Before going into a meeting or an interview or facing a challenge, use this skill to rehearse how you would like the events to transpire. It has a practical and overwhelmingly positive effect on the outcome.

A navy jet pilot used this skill effectively to overcome his fear. He was absolutely terrified at the idea of landing his plane on a heaving, pitching, aircraft carrier. 'Everything was in motion,' he said. 'The ship was tossing up and down, the sea was choppy, the plane was moving around. Trying to get it all together seemed totally impossible.'

Life seems like that sometimes, doesn't it?

A more experienced pilot gave him some advice that solved the problem. 'There's a yellow marker in the centre of the flight deck that appears to stay still. I always line up the nose of the plane towards the marker and fly straight towards it. Ignore the sea. Ignore the movement. Just fly for that yellow marker in the centre.'

Perfect landing every time. That's pretty good advice for living life too. Always have a goal to work toward, and keep your eyes fixed firmly toward it.

Commitment

My children told me a story about commitment. The chicken and the pig were walking to market on market day and they were arguing about who was more important. The chicken said, 'I'm more important, as I provide the eggs for breakfast.' The pig said, 'I'm more important, as I provide the meat'. They argued and argued, and when it looked like no one was going to win, a sudden thought occurred to the pig and he said, 'You are only partly involved in providing the breakfast; with me, it's a full commitment'.

Commitment to your goals will always be tested. Almost as soon as the ink is dry on your goal sheet, your commitment will be tested. Someone or something will stand in the way of you achieving your goal. These objections are called brick walls. Learn to go over the wall, or climb under it, or smash through it. It's just testing you and your commitment to your task. If there isn't a brick wall, then maybe you haven't asked enough of yourself.

You'll notice how quickly the obstacle will dissolve when you are totally committed. Commitment and tenacity are two strong elements in goal setting, enabling you to be empowered and to empower others to succeed with their chosen goals.

*What would you try to achieve if you
believed that it was impossible to fail?*

PAM LANTOS

Choosing a goal and sticking to it changes everything

~~~~~

*If you don't know where you are going,
how can you expect to get there?*

BASIL S. WALSH

Effective Goal Setting

☑ Develop your future memory

☑ The most important thing about goals is having one

☑ Visualise future success

☑ Start moving in a positive direction

☑ Goal setting is about the future, but enables you to live for today

☑ Break your own barriers

☑ Create 'Eternity'

☑ Success equals goal achievement

☑ Set clear specific goals

☑ Develop a detailed plan of action

☑ Match your behaviour with your goals

☑ Watch for limited thinkers

☑ Everything and anything is possible

☑ Pat yourself on the back

☑ Change is constant

☑ Add fire to your goals

☑ Use both sides of the brain

☑ Use visualisation as a tool

☑ The only limitations you have are those you put there

☑ Believe without the evidence

☑ Plant the crop and water it

☑ Commitment

☑ Choosing a goal and sticking to it changes everything

Trusting Yourself

Standing Up Straight

THE VEHICLE

Empowering Yourself
and Others

Elizabeth's story

Johnny was Elizabeth's cousin. They were very close, best friends really. He lived in a little country town about five hours' drive from the city where Elizabeth lived.

This country town had five pubs, two milk bars, five churches, two general stores, a co-operative, an assortment of other businesses and a drapery. This drapery seemed to Elizabeth to be stuck in a time-warp, but she loved it. She loved that the reels of cotton were put away in boxes safely, rather than displayed for the customers to see.

She loved the way the old fashioned shop assisstants were not permitted to give change directly to the customers. They had to place the money from the customers in a cylinder along with an invoice and send it in a vacuum tube which sucked it up noisily to a cashier. The cashier sat high up in the loft in the middle of the building, dispensing change and receipts, like a spider in control of her web.

She had her summer holidays in this country town with Aunt Bess, Uncle Tom and Johnny every year. It was always very exciting because their life was so radically different from her own in the city. It was freer, more open and wilder. It was 1964 and Johnny was going through his rebellious, 'mod' stage, defying authority and hanging out with other 'with it' kids.

One of the more exciting aspects of visiting her relatives was that Johnny's parents owned a pub. Country pubs at that time were a bit rough, so the things she saw and experienced were way out of her normal experience, and she loved it. She loved that a ring barker brought her in a pet lamb to look after for a week, and every day when she went out, the lamb would follow her. She loved to hear the rowdiness in the lounge bar at night as the locals, after too many beers, put their tokens into the juke box and played 'From a Jack to a King' over and over again until Aunt Bess, in desperation, would pull the plug out of the electricity socket just before closing time.

But most of all she loved their nocturnal adventures. Johnny and Elizabeth had formed a kind of a club of like-minded souls who came together for weekly meetings. Although this sounds all very innocent, the meetings were held after midnight down at the showgrounds, on top of the bags of wheat waiting to be transported to the market. These meetings were always catered for by Johnny because of his easy access to liquid refreshments.

Elizabeth and Johnny had to break lots of rules to host these meetings. Climbing down the fire escape was easy; it was the drop at the bottom when they ran out of ladder that was the hard part. And dropping down that six foot expanse was difficult when carrying the stolen stubbies of beer in an old schoolbag.

Getting the beer in the first place required nerves of steel. After 'Last drinks, Gentleman, please' at closing time in the public bar, there was the waiting, listening for the familiar night sounds of Aunty Bess and Uncle Tom getting ready to go to bed. They chattered, seemingly endlessly, as a means of unwinding after a vigorous day serving the general public.

Then came the moment, the strike, which involved stealing the keys to the public bar from the nail in the office, then 'tippytoeing' down the stairs, knowing beforehand exactly where the creaks in the stairs were and favouring the other side. After that came finding the right key for the lock and inserting it, all with the buzz of silence getting louder and louder in their ears, and their hearts pounding faster and faster. Often Johnny did the key-taking by him-

Elizabeth's story

Elizabeth's story

self, telling Elizabeth to meet him outside, because he was frightened to show her how scared he was, in case he cracked and lost his nerve altogether.

They carefully and quietly turned the key to open the door to the public bar. The smell of the just-hosed bar assaulted their senses as they poked their faces around the door. A smell that was to stay with them all their lives, reminding them of fear and risk every time they smelt it, in whatever bar, in whatever town or country. It was the smell of hops, the smell of wet stale bar cloths, the smell of urine wafting from the men's urinal, and the strong pungent smell of sarsaparilla essence coming from the cordial bottles in the corner. Taking the beer was the easy part, and getting out of the bar and back up the stairs to the landing seemed to take no time at all compared with the long, drawn-out time spent getting in.

Then they were on the run, up the alley, down the main street, remembering to hug the dark corners so that they wouldn't be recognised, down the badly lit streets of the country town. They were free, the adrenalin was pumping like the rush of a waterfall, nothing that was to come could surpass that feeling of freedom they both felt at that time but never spoke of.

When they did get caught, when the cook from the hotel kitchen happened to be driving past late one night after visiting her sister, it was terrifying. Never had Elizabeth been so frightened. Her aunt and uncle were so very upset because they were responsible for her during her stay and they had no idea what she and Johnny had been up to.

Johnny was wonderful, he jumped in and said it was all his fault, his idea, his influence that had started their outings, that Elizabeth was completely innocent. Elizabeth appreciated Johnny defending her, she appreciated how he

was protecting her, but something clicked in her head. She felt that if she didn't take equal responsibility, that would be only the beginning of her copping out — not taking responsibility for what she did. Even as a young teenager, she knew that it was the thin edge of the wedge, and if she didn't own up now, it would be the beginning of disempowering herself.

She was given the lecture of a lifetime and sent home. When her father found out, he was upset but also pleased that Elizabeth had taken half the heat, half the responsibility for what she had done. Maybe it didn't make a difference that she had spoken up and admitted what she had done, maybe her behaviour had no real impact on anyone but herself. But Elizabeth realised that truth was the most important thing, that she was going to have a relationship with herself for the rest of her life, and that telling the truth to herself and others had a positive effect on her heart and on her soul.

Elizabeth's story

Decide to be happy,
knowing it's an attitude,
a habit gained from daily practice,
and not a result or payoff.

DENIS WAITLEY

Empowering Yourself and Others

'Empower: the ability or power required for a purpose or task.' Every single person has this power, so why then do many eagerly give it away?

Take responsibility for everything you do

My friend Annie was frustrated with her inability to get things going well in her life and complained that every time she had a problem she could never work out a solution; she was all over the place emotionally. She would telephone me or one of her other friends and complain about the person or thing in her life that was responsible for her unhappiness. She would identify the problem all the time, never taking any responsibility for it nor even seeming as if she honestly wanted it fixed or changed. She just loved to complain.

Whenever something happened that she couldn't handle, she would call someone on the telephone; she would lay all her troubles and woes at her friend's feet. She was very willing to give her problems away to someone else, for them to solve, or give her their sympathy.

It's fine to seek advice, it's wonderful to talk with friends – but not to the extent that you don't check your own inner strength and wisdom first.

She rang me one day to ask for advice, and she didn't get the advice that she thought she wanted. I asked her how long she intended to keep seeking help instead of looking in the mirror at herself and drawing on her own strength. She was more than a little upset about my comments because she felt I was being unsympathetic. But I explained that unless she started to solve her problems and challenges herself, she could spend a lifetime never using her own wisdom and knowledge. She would never truly live her life fully because she would always be seeking help from others, and others don't always know the answers or even have the whole story.

So now, before she grabs the phone, Annie sits quietly, closes her eyes and asks herself what is upsetting her and what she can do to make herself feel better. She then visualises a beautiful white light coming through her hair, surrounding her body and making her feel warm and safe.

Very often, when she finishes this process, she is so busy doing something she thought of as an action plan, or feels so good, that the need to ask advice just isn't there. This is personal empowerment; Annie trusts herself to find a solution for her own problems rather than 'dumping' her problems onto her friends.

Visualisation exercise

Imagine you are sitting on the sand in a secluded beach cove with complete privacy; no one is with you and no one knows of this exquisite place. Look around and take in the surrounding area. Notice the looming cliffs behind you with their yellow and white rocks jutting out to protect the sandy cove. See the whiteness of the beach, the clean, clear perfect grains of sand.

Look out to sea. See how the waves come rolling on to the beach. Listen to the gentle pounding of the surf as it falls upon itself, cascading in a foaming crescendo, then stretches out gently to reach the sand and caress the shoreline with its gentle touch. Smell the freshness in the air, the pureness of the breeze as it wafts across your face. The sun is shining down, spreading its light, creating the most perfect of spring days, warm and clear.

As you are sitting there feeling these magnificent feelings, in your imagination see the white light of the sun pouring down on you and imagine that the light surrounding you creates a feeling of safeness, renewed vigour and confidence. Feel that light surrounding your head and permeating your skin to reach into your mind, your heart and your soul. Feel the cleansing strength of this light.

Sit with this image for a while, and if your mind wanders, just come back to the beach, the waves and the white light. When you feel renewed and refreshed, open your eyes and take that feeling back into whatever you are doing at the time.

Trust your thought pattern

To be empowered, you need to look to yourself first, to listen to your own thoughts, to trust your inner self, to raise the level of trust within yourself. It is impossible to trust others unless you have the ability to trust yourself, to know that no matter what you do, it is right at the time, even if it doesn't always appear that way.

I met a businessman at a luncheon. He was a bit like Annie. I had known David for the time it took to eat the first course and he was telling me all about his business, and particularly about how he didn't trust his staff. They were lazy and dishonest with the hours they said they worked, and although he didn't know for sure, he was certain that they were taking his stock, that they were stealing from him.

David was bitter and angry, and because of this bitterness and anger, his vision was being clouded by how he felt. I'm not saying that the things he complained about weren't happening, but with his frame of mind, he had very little chance of changing them. They were becoming a self-fulfilling prophecy.

I talked with him about why he had started his business and why he created a business with a large staff. He told me that he had never intended to have so many people working for him, but the business had just grown like crazy. He never really trusted his own skills in communicating with people and asking them to do things, he said.

It was evident that David would never have the ability to manage if he didn't first start with himself. He needed to start believing in himself and building his personal leadership skills so that he could start directing his team and monitoring their performance, the first steps to trusting them.

There is a saying that goes like this: 'Trust the universe, but tether your camel', loosely translated in modern times as: 'Trust the world, but lock your car'. The actor Michelle Pfeiffer often quotes her father's words to her, 'Trust everyone, but cut the cards'.

In David's case he needed to trust his people, but he needed also to put measures of assessment into place so that he could measure their behaviour against their performance standards and give them feedback about their work and their progress.

A measure I suggested to David that really works, whether in the work place, or with special-interest groups, or with sporting teams or with your family, is a process called 'One on Ones'. It is a simple goal-setting exercise whereby you and the person with whom you will do this 'One on One' make time every six weeks to create and write down your goals for the next six weeks, in a supportive and friendly environment. Somewhere quiet where there will be no disturbances or interruptions is essential. A 'One on One' done with interruptions is hardly worth doing, as the person with whom you are doing it will believe you do not value them or their time.

Guidelines to achieve effective 'One on Ones'

◆ *Keep the goals simple and achievable*

◆ *Define the time span for goals and action and commit it to writing*

◆ *Participants write their own goals in their own handwriting*

◆ *Make sure the person 'wins' and achieves*

◆ *Use this as a process for recognising each others' achievements*

◆ *Use the time to reinforce behaviour matching goals*

◆ *Time frame needs to be 20 to 30 minutes duration (no longer)*

◆ *Always set a time for the next 'One on One' at the end of the last one*

◆ *Offer to support, in appropriate ways, the other person*

The benefits of using this communication process are many. It makes your team think about what they want over a short, measurable time frame. You will share ideas that you may not have the time or the inclination to do under normal circumstances. You will make a commitment to some short-term goals and have the means to evaluate the progress towards those goals, as a team. It is a process that really helps people to convert ideas into action, but mostly it empowers the individual to achieve, to make decisions and to work towards a measurable target.

On the following page is an example of a 'One on One' a console operator in a service station wrote about her goals and action plan.

> *Treat people as if they were what they ought to be, and help them become what they are capable of being...*
>
> JOHANN WOLFGANG VON GOETHE

Today's date: 24/09   *Date in six weeks: 05/11*

GOALS/OBJECTIVES/TARGETS/AIMS

(Things that will turn problems around/allow you to achieve in your work/create effective teamwork/create personal job satisfaction)

1. *Learn more about the difference between oils for cars and motorbikes*
2. *Improve customer service*
3. *Learn more about places of interest in our area*
4. *Cut down on waste*
5. *Wear uniform proudly*
6. *Work effectively and get everything done*

ACTION PLAN TO ACHIEVE

(Short-term, specific action you can take to achieve these goals, action which will match your behaviour to the goals)

1. *Book into oil seminar next month! Read manual about oils – 1 page a day*
2a. *Smile and greet customers consistently*
2b. *Ask if customer needs help with anything (e.g. if looking at accessories stand)*
3a. *Give directions to places and point out places of interest in that area (e.g. wildlife park, beaches)*
3b. *Read information brochures on the area. If someone says they went to an attraction, ask them what they thought of it*
4a. *Think before throwing something out*
4b. *Use directed amounts of cleaning products*
5. *Wash and iron uniform the night before, clean shoes every second day*
6a. *Clean counter as soon as spills occur. Stock up on sugar etc, to fill up refrigerated cakes*
6b. *Complete tasks from cleaning roster each shift*

The difference between the goal and the action is that the goal is the target, and the action is what gets you to this target. The action also becomes your behaviour. If you have an action plan in place, your behaviour will always match your goal. For instance, if your goal is to upgrade your presentation, the way you look, the way you dress, you need to be prepared to do something toward this regularly, on a daily basis, such as clean your shoes or plan your wardrobe for the next day. By doing this, you will be able to achieve your goal.

I have consulted with a team whose business is selling oil and gas and fast food. They have a service station on the coast road between Noosa and Brisbane, in Queensland, Australia. They call themselves Magnet Mobil Fast Food. They do this because they are so committed to excellence in customer service that their *vision* is to be a *magnet* to people who visit, experience and buy from them the range of goods and services they provide. They aim to be so good in customer service that people can't help but be drawn back to them again and again.

It's a gutsy statement to make, Magnet Mobil, but they make it because they believe in *integrity based customer service*, which begins with giving themselves great customer service, then giving their fellow team members great customer service. It's not until they can show this commitment to serving each other that they then believe they have the right to serve the consumer or the end user with excellent customer service.

They believe that the 'One on One' process has been the key to the success of this effective team customer service, that these simple six-weekly goal-setting exercises provide the environment for each member of their team to better themselves, their performance and their relationship with all their team members.

The Magnet team decided that for their 'One on Ones' to be effective they would need to have a group of team leaders who implemented this process with their teams. They have six team leaders, and each team leader is responsible for five to 10 people (depending on the size of their teams). Each leader participates in the process with each team member every six weeks. At that time they evaluate progress, create a new list of goals and share each other's objectives, successes and failures. They re-evaluate, reset and move on, always in a forward direction.

I know that whenever my training company has implemented this simple process and it has been followed through, its effectiveness has improved the productivity, the relationships between people and the culture of the company in a very positive way. I also encourage you to set a time every six weeks to do this 'One on One' process with your children, to help them to learn this valuable empowerment skill.

Here is an example of a 'One on One' with a teenage girl:

Today's date 26/05   Date in six weeks: 07/07

GOALS/OBJECTIVES/TARGETS/AIMS
(Things that will turn problems around/allow you to achieve in your work/create effective teamwork/create personal job satisfaction)
1.   *Improve schoolwork*
2.   *Understand maths more*
3.   *Get on with Dad*
4.   *Be more positive*
5.   *Have a happy relationship with John B*

ACTION PLAN TO ACHIEVE
(Short-term, specific action you can take to achieve these goals, action which will match your behaviour to the goals)
1.   *Set study schedule at 3 hours per night Mon–Fri*
2.   *Ask for more help from teacher/tutor*
3.   *Be pleasant at dinner time, be polite; be caring; understand Dad's perspective more*
4.   *Work on my self esteem; use visualisation every night; focus on my good points; forgive myself for my mistakes*
5.   *Be a good listener; speak clearly about my needs; be kind and forgiving*

Life can't go according to plan
if there is no plan

TAMMIE BENNETT

Sandy, a teenage schoolgirl who works part-time in a clothing store, asked me how she could write her 'One on One'. She had no problems with the goal-setting section – she knew what she wanted; but she was unsure of how to go about getting it.

Her goals were much like those of the teenage girl above: to improve her schoolwork, to be more positive about herself, and to enjoy the company of her friends. However, it wasn't just a matter of wanting to 'get on with Dad'; her problem seemed bigger than that of the teenage girl in the above example. Her problem was her stepfather. This man hadn't come into her life by her design but by her mother's. This man believed he had the right to tell her what and when to do things, and took up all of her beautiful mother's time and left little time for her mother to spend with her.

He was always grumpy, especially when he came home from work. He worked as an ambulance driver and when he came home at night he was always short with her, pushing her away, telling her to go to her room, that he needed to be alone, away from all the kids for a while.

Whenever she did anything for him or her mother, he was always critical. He was always so hard to please. She resented his existence. She secretly wished that her mother would see what an evil person he was and leave him, as she had left Sandy's real dad.

All this story came flooding out, every painful word. After Sandy had finished relating her view of her home life, it surprised me that she wanted to set a goal about her stepfather at all. But she knew in her heart that if she did not take conscious action about it, it would only get worse. Brave girl! So she set about the business of writing her action plan to achieve her goal of getting on with her stepfather. This is what she decided to do in her action plan:

67

◆ *Schedule my study time so that it coincides with my stepfather's arrival home.*

◆ *Be aware of my stepfather's relationship with his father; be more compassionate towards him (because in fact he is only replicating how he was treated by his dad), and be more understanding about this.*

◆ *Stand back from the situation when I am being criticised and detach myself from it rather than attack back. See it as being more about him than about me and do not react negatively.*

◆ *Offer to help more around the house, be the first to offer help.*

◆ *Stop the hate I feel for him in my head (it feels like it is doing me more damage anyway). I will let go of this horrible feeling and replace it with feelings of openness toward him.*

◆ *Stay out of the arguments that the other children have with him. Let them sort it out with him directly, rather than trying to save the situation all the time.*

These clear, specific, short-term actions, Sandy believed, would bring about the behaviour that would help her to turn the tide with her stepfather.

Last time I spoke with her, she looked like a new person. Her posture was more erect, her confidence when speaking with me had changed for the better, everything about her had matured. I asked how she was going with her goals and action plan, and she beamed. Yes, she had improved her relationship with her stepfather. He was still grumpy and irritable sometimes, she said, but he was treating her with much more respect, concern and interest.

The thing that she was most pleased about was her improved relationship with her mother. Her mother had seen just how much she had changed her attitude and was enormously proud and grateful for her support. Somehow they had become allies and friends again and this made Sandy so very happy.

Sandy decided to show her mother her goal and action sheet and they decided to do this 'One on One' process together as mother and daughter every four weeks, and to review it and reset goals and action regularly. If it could work with Sandy's relationship with her stepfather, they firmly believed that it could work with any goals.

Empower others and you empower yourself

Whether at work, in your family, in a sporting or special-interest group, give your team the opportunity to have successes and failures. There is the risk when you give others the power to make their own decisions and act upon them that they will make mistakes; it is part of the learning process. If you don't give your team this responsibility and then support and monitor it, you are going to pay the price. The price is that you will end up with a team of people who will only go so far with decisions; they will be afraid to try anything new or different for fear of being reprimanded or reproached. The 'One on One' process will give you a vehicle to enable them to make goals, to monitor them and to appraise their performance.

I met Berry through a training program I was running for her company. The program was about team building and we were at the last stage of the process: the implementation of the 'One on One' process. Berry always sat up the back of the room for our sessions, never really getting involved, never really committing herself to the general discussion, always holding back. I am a great believer in respect of the individual, and the individual's right to his or her values and beliefs, so in no way would I push Berry to participate more in these sessions than she was prepared to.

My job was to provide skills and tools to help the team to put the new vision of the company into place and to help them to work more effectively as a team and respect themselves and each other in achieving this vision. But things got a little tricky in the last session when I was introducing the team to the 'One on One' process and asking them to try this process by actually sitting in groups of two, pairing with someone with whom they worked closely. Berry became very agitated. She refused to talk to her workmate about the goals they could set, and actually turned her back on the group and started to doodle on her worksheet.

I gently asked her to participate, just to help her workmate Ann with the exercise. Ann was as keen as mustard to do the exercise, but without Berry's help it would be difficult for Ann to participate, as there was no one else for her to partner.

Berry refused to do this. I thanked her for speaking her mind and told her that she was free to leave the session whenever she wanted. She did, but not before she told me and the rest of the team what a stupid idea goal setting was, how it never worked; it would never work here in this company, and it would never solve the problems of this company as nobody cared and nothing would change.

After she left, the rest of the group had a general discussion and decided that it was a worthwhile process and to continue. The general manager, Danny, who had been present throughout, decided to take on Berry as his personal responsibility and was hopeful that he would convince Berry to participate in the 'One on One' process so that the whole team could benefit from this exciting procedure.

I spoke to Danny a week later. He was despondent. He had approached Berry twice in the previous week and found himself stonewalled in relation to her setting goals. He was determined to keep trying, however.

Two weeks later he rang me, excited about the overall progress of goal setting. It was having an enormously positive impact on his team, his sales figures were up since the program, the teams were talking to each other about customer satisfaction, and his reception area had taken on an exceptionally welcoming ambience. But he saved the best till last. Berry had started her

'One on One' goalsetting process with him a week before and had already achieved everything on her sheet.

Danny had redesigned the goal sheet using his words and making it relevant to his business, a computer software supply company. He had asked for her input about her problems, and he had told her how valuable her involvement in the program was. Danny also showed Berry how well the rest of the team were doing with the exercise and impressed her with the benefits to be gained from using goal setting.

Berry became the most enthusiastic user of goal setting in the company and she spread that enthusiasm to the other team members. Because they had witnessed her original rejection of the program, the team was delighted that she was the one now enthusing them over targets and using this process as a means of problem solving. But most of all, they were happy she had decided to join the team effort in this exciting process.

The acid test in empowering others is: could your business or family or group run without you if you needed to leave the country for six months? Making people dependent upon you is not empowering; it's fear-based and doesn't lead to group or individual effectiveness. Trusting that your team will give it their best shot and monitoring their progress on a regular basis will create a team of willing and creative participants.

When I was growing up in the country, there was a nursing home for the elderly nearby run by its owner, Mr Theodore. I grew up hearing the townsfolk say they would rather leave the district than end their lives under the tyranny of Mr Theodore. He ran the home like a military camp, every task was done precisely a certain way. If any of his staff spent any time with the residents, he felt that was time wasted and they would be reprimanded. The sheets were threadbare but the staff were afraid to make the beds with new ones, sitting on shelves in the cupboard, for fear of inciting the wrath of the feared Mr Theodore.

You might say this couldn't happen now, in this day and age. Well it is still occurring in businesses, in people's homes and people's minds. We, as individuals, can help prevent it by empowering others on a one-to-one basis, and by raising our individual level of trust.

It is all too easy to blame the government, the system, the bosses, with all the problems of the land. Yes, they are responsible for what they do, but so are we. I have heard the expression, 'One person cannot change the world'. I don't believe that this is true. If enough 'one persons' empower themselves – through taking responsibility for themselves, by making decisions and being responsible for their outcome, by setting goals and matching their action and their behaviour to those goals – then enough 'one people' will change the world into a place where caring and fairness are the standards that our lives are based upon.

Expect success

In a family, how long do parents give their child to learn to walk? Six months? Six years? They don't set a time limit. They naturally expect the child to walk, and that's what invariably happens. And they certainly don't give up on the child if he or she stumbles at first.

Kimberley is a six-year-old girl and she expects to do well at her school's spell-o-thon. Why? She practises every day and she expects success because her mother expects she will do her best. Her father expects she will do well and supports her. Her grandparents feel the same way.

The child believes without having the evidence in front of her. There are no 'ifs', 'maybes' or 'perhaps' about it. Why should she 'expect' anything but her best? Can you be like this with the people you work with? Can you place enough confidence in them? If you place the confidence in them, they'll have the capacity to live up to it.

So you need to have more of a long-range plan for your teams, like you do for your family. Give your team standards to reach and then monitor them. When they fall, like the child learning to walk, help them up, encourage them, give them the next target to go for. Encourage them like Kimberley was encouraged; your attitude to your people directly affects their performance.

I was giving a training program to a real estate company recently; they spoke of their salespeople as costing the company $25 000 to $80 000 a year, rather than looking at that team as a valuable resource bringing in hundreds of thousands of dollars worth of business a year. Yet, if a potential client walked into their office and offered to spend half a million dollars on a property that was listed with them, they would treat that client like a long lost son. They would make that client comfortable, offer coffee, ask about his or her interests.

Every salesperson in that company is capable of bringing in at least that much business, and how are they treated? Are they seen and treated as 'half million dollar' clients? It is essential to treat the 'internal' customer, your teams and their teams, with the same integrity, the same value, as the 'external' customer. That's what *integrity based customer service* is all about, treating the *internal customer* as well as the external customer.

Integrity based customer service

The philosophy behind *integrity based customer service* is that to achieve the very best in service for your customers, or on a personal level with friends, you must be prepared to give yourself excellence in customer service first in order to develop a strong self value. Match your self value with your self image by giving yourself strong positive self talk. Serving yourself also means having a commitment to your wellness, to match your behaviour with your goal by keeping a balanced diet, getting enough sleep, giving yourself a balanced life with work and play, family and friends.

Once you have given yourself great customer service, the next customer to serve is the internal customer, your teams and their team members or your family. Your family is a vital part of the team. Give your internal team praise or reprimand them at the time of achievement or making a mistake, implementing the 'One on One' process to maintain the lines of effective communication.

Then, and only then, do you have the right to serve the end user, the customer or, on a personal level, your friends. This is done through adding value to what you do with this person, by giving more than the expected level of service and by going out of your way to do or say something special for that person. It is about building better business and relationships, through giving more. When the situation arises, it means dealing effectively with difficult people or people who have problems, and converting their problems quickly into projects, thus creating solutions.

Having a value-added attitude to yourself, to the team (including your family), and to the customer gives an organisation heart. By giving these three circles equal attention, you are creating the heart of a business.

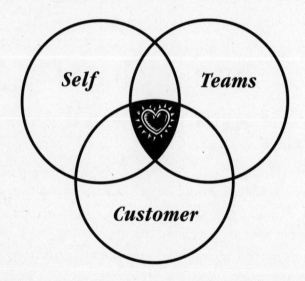

Dealing with yourself and others with integrity means catching yourself and others in the act of doing things right. Not waiting until you find something wrong. Find more of what is going right, because in reality the true situation is that most of what happens *is* right.

Open up every meeting with a positive statement on an achievement of the week, no matter how insignificant it may be. Every person at the meeting should have a minute or two to contribute something positive they've done or something positive they've learnt about their job since the previous meeting.

Catch people doing things right and tell them

~~~~~~~

Where praise is due, don't be afraid to give it, and make sure it goes to the right person. It's no good telling others in your team about what a great worker James is, if James never hears it. Be specific in your praise. Many people just don't know which things they're doing right, so if you can point these out and positively reinforce them, they will probably continue doing these things. You can slap James on the back and tell him, 'Great job, James', and he'll probably have no idea of the specific achievement you're talking about.

Don't save it up, give it when it's due. There is no point in addressing the team once a year with an inspirational message if that is the last thing they'll hear from you till the next office Christmas party. End-of-year bonuses and incentive schemes are one way of showing management's appreciation of good work, but the right word at the right time can be more effective.

In any environment – family, sporting club, social club or business – recognition is a great motivation. Find out just what makes others feel good about themselves and concentrate on that. Effective praise makes people more confident and more responsible. And it makes the team more fun and alive, and increases everyone's productivity.

There is always at least one hard-nosed cynic out there saying, 'Yes, that's all very well, but if I praise others all the time they will get a big head.' No, not if the praise is legitimate, honest and at the point of, or close to, the time when they did whatever it was that was right.

There are going to be times when people make mistakes, when the ship founders on the rocks of negligence or incompetence, when some person simply forgets all about a report they promised, and the people they work with have to take up the slack. This happened with Nathan's team leader, Sonya, who noticed that the information for a report she had asked Nathan to write was still in rough form in his in-tray after 5.00 pm. Nathan had obviously gone for the day and had forgotten to do it, and the deadline was for first thing in the morning. As soon as she saw it she knew that she would have to work back to get it done, and she was mad, because she had to give up time with her family that she had promised them and work back two hours writing the report to have it ready by 9.00 am the next morning.

The next day, Nathan wandered in to Sonya's office still totally oblivious to his mistake. It would be an understatement to describe Sonya as angry, she passed angry at about 7.00 pm the previous night. So how does a situation like this relate to positive programming?

For a start, there's nothing wrong with Sonya being angry. She had a right to be angry. She earned that right the night before when she worked back to solve the problem. So she was angry. But like praise, effective reprimand needs to be specific and clear. It is not an opportunity to drag up every little problem from the past two years. Effective reprimand is about fixing the immediate problem so it won't happen again.

Go to the source of the problem and fix it

Sonya tackled the situation at hand, saying, 'I am incredibly angry with you, Nathan. You forgot all about that report and I had to work back till after seven o'clock last night on an evening I was planning to spend with my family. You knew that report had to be ready by nine this morning. I am very disappointed with your behaviour.'

There was no point in name calling. There was no point in making Nathan the target of all the anger for the whole of her lifetime, just in relation to the current situation. Sonya got it out of her system and made sure her anger was directed at the right person, and for the right reasons. She used the reprimand to fix the problem with the person responsible. It didn't get her time back with her family, but it is unlikely Nathan will make that same mistake again.

Check yourself for the real reason you are angry

An office manager called Robert told the following story against himself at a gathering one evening. He enjoyed going to lunch. He would rather sit at the coffee shop for an hour or so than grab a sandwich at work. He was a good manager and when he noticed that many of his team were following his example and getting back to work late every now and then, he decided to set the standard and stay in for lunch and have a sandwich with his team.

This lasted for about a week. He had to take an out-of-town client to lunch and when he left the restaurant at 3.30 pm he was feeling very angry with himself for being late. He hurried a little too much for his own good coming back to the office and went through a radar trap, going over the speed limit. With the time at 3.45 pm and a costly speeding ticket in his pocket, he walked back into the office kicking himself mercilessly.

There was so much anger in him, he had to let it out somewhere, and his assistant happened to be the handiest person around. 'Where are those figures you promised me this afternoon? Why aren't they on my desk?' yelled Robert.

'Well, you said that you didn't need them till tomorrow...' replied Robert's assistant, Tammy.

And do you know what Robert said? 'I don't care what I told you, I want those figures now.'

So Tammy walked away feeling very hard done by. There at her desk, proofreading a newsletter, sat her colleague, Scott. 'Robert wants those figures on his desk now. Perhaps if you spent less time on less important things, you would have helped me have those to him by now.'

Scott stomped off to ask the accountant where the figures were, and passed on his anger to her about not having given the information to him earlier. The accountant had not been given a deadline to work to. She had no idea that these figures were urgent, and in fact they weren't; she was just at the end of the line. She got the figures ready but went home feeling aggrieved at being given a hard time about something that was not her responsibility. She was still frustrated when she walked through the door and she yelled at her teenage daughter for the messiness of the house.

Now Tess, the accountant's daughter, was upset. She hated her mother coming home from work in a bad mood. Sitting innocently, dreaming of mice and sardines, was the cat, and because Tess was angry she pushed the cat aside as she stormed off to her room.

Now wouldn't it have made a lot more sense for Robert to have gone straight to Tess's home and 'kicked her cat' in the first place. He'd have gotten rid of his anger, and all the innocent bystanders, bar the cat, would have been spared.

Next time you're angry about a situation, check yourself for the real reason and be honest with yourself. Don't pass it on to innocent bystanders. Next time someone is angry with you, remember it may not be you they are mad at. Someone has probably just 'kicked their cat'.

All the new technology and technological developments in the world won't help people work as a team. As individuals, each person in the team is responsible for successful team operation, responsible for telling the truth directly to the person or people concerned – not going to others and gossiping or endlessly asking their opinion – responsible for going and fixing the problem directly.

Our team, whether at home or at work, is capable of much more than any of us believe, more than the evidence may suggest. All it takes is a little positive input on our part – consistent, supportive behaviour – and our team will achieve its wildest dreams.

Our team, whether at home or at work,
is capable of much more than any of us believe –
more than evidence may suggest.

ANON

Act upon what you know now

Human nature is such that you want to have *all* the information before making a decision, but you never will. It is important to make decisions, trusting your current wisdom, your current information and knowledge as well as your gut feelings. You will never have all the information. Your gut feel, your personal wisdom, is everything you have seen or heard or emotionally felt, recorded in your head, your heart and your soul. It is all there, you haven't missed anything and now you need to trust it. Listen to it, feel it, do what it says. In its pure form, it will never let you down.

I watched Tommy Emmanuel, acclaimed guitarist, interviewed on television. He talked of how he listened to his gut feel. During a tour of Europe in 1987, he saw a lovely girl in the front row. He said that she filled him with so much love that it was supernatural. At the end of the set, he jumped into the audience to find her, but she had disappeared.

By chance, he met her later in the evening and invited her for a meal. Because he had only just arrived in Europe, he had no local currency to pay for the meal. To add insult to injury, she didn't even remember him as the guitarist from the concert. She ended up paying for their meal and dropped him at his hotel at four in the morning, not interested in seeing him again. He pestered her for her phone number, and within the hour was waking her up to ask her out for breakfast. Three months later he proposed and was accepted.

He said that he had never done anything like that in his life. 'But there are certain points in your life when you have to take risks. The difference between achievers and non-achievers is that when the road curves and you can't see what's ahead, achievers keep going.'

Emmanuel took responsibility for an idea and followed it through; his gut feel worked. You need to take responsibility for everything you create, not blame or judge others for what they did or didn't do. You create your own reality, you are responsible for what is in your life, consciously or subconsciously. What freedom it is to embrace this and then recreate what you want!

If you have created the mess you are in, then you can recreate anything else just as effectively

~~~~~~

You create both the mess and the happiness in your life, by your thoughts. Your thoughts become matter and then become your reality. What is your thought pattern right now? Is your thought pattern serving you by creating the kind of environment around you that you desire, or are you serving some old negative thought pattern that you have brought forward into your life from a place you never want to go back to. Clean up the thought pattern and make it live for you, not you live for it.

In cleaning up your thought pattern you will then be ready to clean up the way in which you treat others, to treat others as you would like to be treated yourself. You no doubt heard this on your mother's knee, or at school, or from a kind neighbour. Somewhere, you were given this great knowledge and, basically, it is the greatest knowledge there is.

Judge others and you judge yourself

~~~~~~

When we meet people for the first time we sometimes judge them harshly. We watch people walking along the street and put them in a category that sometimes bears no resemblance to their true selves. Judging other people often takes the heat off ourselves. We can criticise others for not being perfect, or for their humanness. Often people who criticise others harshly do not trust themselves and are just filling their lives up with negative criticism so that they can remain aloof or not have to look at their own behaviour and clean up their own backyards.

I met Karl at the beginning of a team-building weekend I was facilitating for the key people of a global chemical company. Karl was the manager of the group participating and I noticed that he moved his chair away from the main table. We had set up the room with tables and chairs laid out in a square shape so that everyone would feel equal at the meeting, to create an atmosphere where each participant would feel they could contribute equally.

I was more than a little perturbed when he indicated he was going to sit away from the group, and I said so. His reply was '...my best role is as a critic. I'll be able to judge people's reactions and give you feedback about the program more easily if I'm not involved directly.'

I was surprised and disappointed, as his company was paying me a professional fee to build the team, including him. If they needed a critical assessmant of me, surely it should have been done before I even got the job, not during the program. I would have loved for him to give me a running commentary during the breaks as to how he saw things and how I could fine tune the program, but he could have done that without separating himself from the rest of his team. I could see what kind of a visual impact his separating himself from the group had on them, but there was no changing his mind.

I promise you: criticise me he did, with enormous gusto and enthusiasm. In fact, it made me wonder if he had even been in the room during the program, because we talked about communication and feedback and how it needs to be a balance of 80 per cent positive and 20 per cent fixing problems to be effective, not the other way around.

The reason he judged others so harshly was so that he could disguise his insecurity about himself from the team. Often the best form of defence is attack, and Karl was an expert at it.

When we are kind to others, notice what they are doing right and help them to build on that, they have a chance to exceed their own expectations. It does not take a mental giant to find mistakes, but it does take enormous kindness to notice the good things and comment on them.

Create random acts of kindness

Acts of kindness are like precious starfish in the deep blue ocean of life – rare, valuable. But we get back what we put out in life, fair and square. Look around you, look what you have created in your relationships, friendships and communications. They are a direct result of what you have put into them by way of time, energy, kindness, compassion and caring. Creating acts of kindness is about what you are putting out and how kind you are prepared to be.

A random act of kindness can be almost anything, but usually it's when you do more for someone else than either of you was expecting, when you put aside your fears and insecurities and are better than yourself, thinking more of someone else than of yourself.

When I was pregnant, I remember a kind but very frail old man giving up his seat to me on a train. I remember thinking at the time that even in my large state I was more robust than he was, but I accepted his kindness graciously, just the same.

I remember once arriving late after a long and dusty day's drive in the Australian outback. I stumbled into a motel well after the kitchen was closed, asking if there was a possibility of getting a bite to eat, a sandwich or something light, feeling it was a lost cause because of the lateness and the general rules of such places.

The joy, relief and overwhelming kindness I felt when the night clerk said, 'I can see you've had a long and dusty drive, Luv, you settle in to your room and I'll bring you over a meal just like your Mum would make and that'll set you right.' I still get a lump in my throat when I remember her generosity and the warmth of her gesture.

My mother talks of the gestures of kindness she has witnessed over the years, particularly during the depression of the 1930s. To support their families, men left the cities and went out into the country looking for work, doing whatever they could find so that they could send something back to keep their families alive during a time of enormous shortages and privations. Country people who had little for themselves would happily share their meagre meals with complete strangers, caring for them for a short time with great kindness.

People from that generation were great givers, but because of their fierce independence and need to be self sufficient many did not learn the gracious art of receiving as well as they could. Betty was just such a product of her environment. She was a great giver, but more than a great giver, she was almost a sacrificer. She was always going out of her way to be kind to others. This was a wonderful thing and others soon learnt not only to expect it but to take advantage of it. Betty was always the person at work who would take the extra shift to help one of her workmates out because they had a date or a sick child, but Betty was fast becoming a martyr.

Whenever anyone else tried to do anything for her she said, 'No, I'm okay, I'm fine, don't worry about me', and wouldn't accept any kindness. She was close to burnout and was starting to resent others around her, with their constant demands, for not caring enough about her.

In short, being kind to others is only really honest if we give others the opportunity to reciprocate. Sacrificing for others is not honest because it cuts the circle of completeness. The circle of kindness is only complete when we have the courage to give and receive equally, otherwise it can become both manipulative and dissatisfying.

Being kind allows you to access something that is bigger than yourself, allows you to be a bit better than you normally are. You have that capacity, but you may not be accessing it to the fullest.

Limitations are self made

~~~

The only limits are, as always, those of vision.

JAMES BROUGHTON

Becoming Empowered

☑ Take responsibility for everything you do

☑ Trust your thought pattern

☑ Empower others and you empower yourself

☑ Expect success

☑ Integrity based customer service

☑ Catch people doing things right and tell them

☑ Go to the source of the problem and fix it

☑ Check yourself for the real reason you are angry

☑ Act upon what you know now

☑ If you have created the mess you are in, then you can
   re-create anything else just as effectively

☑ Judge others and you judge yourself

☑ Create random acts of kindness

☑ Limitations are self made

Change

*Change Is an Opportunity
Sometimes Disguised as a Threat*

THE VEHICLE

How to Use Change as a Positive
for Personal Growth

Elizabeth's story

The first time Elizabeth saw Joel he was standing at the tuckshop at school. He was head and shoulders above the rest of the people there and she guessed that he was about six feet two. He was also *drop dead* gorgeous – blond, soft, clean hair and sparkling azure blue eyes with a twinkle in them that made you feel that when you were around him, you were having fun.

Elizabeth fell in love with him immediately. It was the first time for her, so the strength of her desire was a big surprise to her. They became friends then lovers, young love at its most pure and powerful. Virgins, the both of them, bound up in the intensity of first love as if they had invented it.

The pleasure of it all: the discovery of each other's bodies, each other's minds and thinking, and of each other's friendship. The thing they loved to do the most was to meet under the protection of the old bridge. The countryside was green and lush at that time of the year, with the river flowing languidly through it. Over the river, standing firm and strong, was a beautiful old grey bridge, originally built as a toll bridge. The paint peeling from the underneath section only served to give it more character and, seemingly, more shelter.

It was their shelter, their hideaway, the place where they chose to release their unbridled passion; the place where intimacy, previously unknown to them both, was shared and recreated in touch, in heart and in soul. The first night they kissed under the bridge and held each other tight, Elizabeth felt she would never lose the smell of him from her body.

So when Elizabeth noticed a withdrawal of Joel's affection for her, it was as if a plug had been pulled – that feeling of being left in the bath when all the water has gone down the plug hole and you are still there, cold, shivering and alone.

She couldn't gain his love back; she tried, but nothing she could do could make it the way it was. It wasn't until she saw him with Kim that she understood why; he had transferred all his affection for her on to Kim. It was over, there was no going back.

Elizabeth got angry, she became resentful, she cried so hard that she thought she would be empty inside. Nothing would stop the hurt she was feeling. She grieved well, she got into sadness with both feet, and when she had enough of it, she let go. Eventually she saw the experience as beautiful and wonderful and was able to go on to other loves and life and other changes, but this love was to be the one that taught her more than any of the others that followed. It taught her that after you have done everything positive that you can and you still can't change something back, you have to let go and move on.

Elizabeth's story

If one desires a change,
one must be that change
before that change can take place.

GITA BELLIN

How to Use Change as a Positive for Personal Growth

We've just experienced a decade of the most incredible change in human history. Everywhere you look, new technology is changing the face of the world. New ideas and new approaches are revolutionising industry, commerce, communications and the way we all live. We've changed the world, and so we must change too: the way we relate to each other; the way we communicate; the way we manage people. Just as you'd expect the modern word processor to be more efficient and more productive than the old-fashioned typewriter, you can expect to be more efficient, more productive, more successful.

Look at the 'clean' silicon chip. Clean and unprogrammed, it's useless. You can't expect it to perform until the right circuits and the right programs have been etched into it. The human brain is not so very different. We're all born with a clean chip, and as we grow older, various programs are etched into our make-up by our parents, our schooling, by our environment in general.

When old words die out on the tongue, new melodies break forth from the heart; & where old tracks are lost, new country is revealed with its wonders.

RABINDRANATH TAGORE

Desire creates the power for change

~~~

A lot of that programming is negative. You are taught your limitations – what not to do – very early in life, and learn to do only what is expected and accepted. Much of our reaction to change is a result of this programming, and because of this, instead of embracing change as exciting, as challenging, we view it as a threat, as negative, as a hindrance, rather than looking at it as the opportunity it really is.

> *The world is too big for us. There is too much doing; too many crimes, casualties, violence and excitement. Try as you will, you get behind the race in spite of yourself. It is an incessant strain to keep pace and still you lose ground. Science empties its discoveries on you so fast that you stagger beneath them in hopeless bewilderment. The political world witnesses new scenes so rapidly that you are out of breath trying to keep up with them. Everything is high pressure. Human nature cannot endure much more.*

This is an extract from an article written about change and changing technology; it appeared in the *Atlantic Journal* nearly 150 years ago.

Recognise change as an opportunity

~~~

Change comes in many forms during a lifetime. Children can experience life-changing pain through the divorce of their parents. Often children think it was somehow their fault, something they did or didn't do to make it better for their parents. Children can also experience the pain of change through moving houses or moving schools.

Adults can experience the same discomfort and pain from these experiences. A colleague recently put her house on the market and she and her husband woke up automatically every morning at 2.30 am with mild anxiety, both wondering if they had made the right decision. This is a normal, healthy reaction to change.

You can experience five to 50 or more big changes in your lifetime, ranging from coping with a new position in the workforce, to losing your job, to the death of someone close to you, or something as simple as the corner shop moving location and having to change your mindset to go to a different location. One of the most consistent things in life is change, and it is your ability not just to keep up with these changes but to be active about change that contributes enormously to your success in life. Many people fear success because they fear the change that they know will inevitably go with it.

Be proactive about change

Your conditioning can hold you back from being proactive about change. By the age of four, about 50 per cent of your conditioning has taken place. Between the ages of four and eight, a further 30 per cent takes place. By the age of 14, 90 per cent of your basic conditioning – your reactions and your programming towards life – has already occurred. So if you are 24, 90 per cent of your reactions have been the same for 10 years. If you are 34, for 20 years, and if you are 74, for 60 years. It's no wonder that you resist change.

A young girl, her name is Jenny, told me a story about her family recently. They were very *anti*-change; tradition and rules played a large part in her family culture. Every Sunday her mother would have a roast. Every Sunday her grandmother and her great grandmother would attend this family occasion.

You could absolutely guarantee what would be served to you every Sunday lunch: roast beef, roast potatoes, sweet potatoes, peas in mint sauce, beans, cauliflower, gravy made from the juices from the roast beef pan, and home-made horseradish sauce. The roast would be served exactly at one o'clock, all the best cutlery, crockery and glassware were laid on the table, and the roast was always cooked in two pieces and served on a large antique platter. Everybody had their places set especially for them and Jenny always sat exactly in the same place every week; in fact, everyone sat in the exact same places every time they came for Sunday lunch.

Jenny often wondered about the roast. Why was it always cut in two before it was put into the oven? She asked her mother, who had been cooking it for all the seven years since Jenny had been born, 'Mummy, why do you always cut the roast in half to cook it?'

Her mother looked startled and said, 'Why, Jenny, I really have no idea. My mother always did it like this and I have always believed that that's just the way it's done. Mother, why did you always do it this way?' Jenny's grandmother looked quizzically at her mother, the great grandmother, at the table, and this is what the great grandmother said:

> Why, I thought you understood; fancy, after all these years, and you never understood. It was because when my husband and I were first married, conditions were pretty tough in the outback back then and your Pa made me a makeshift oven; it was pretty small, but it did the job right enough. But I had to cut the big Sunday roast in two to fit it in when all the drovers would ride for miles to our table for their one cooked meal for the week. I guess it just stayed with me as a sort of a habit.

Conditioning is doing something in a certain way just because it has always been done that way. Doing something because it has always been done that way isn't necessarily the best or the most appropriate way to do it now. Examine your reaction to change. Are you reacting in this way because it goes against the way you have always done such things in the past? If so, choose to change your reactions, and change the way you do things to suit the tasks and yourself – don't follow tradition for tradition's sake. You always have a choice.

Just because you have always done it this way doesn't make it the most appropriate way now

Traditionally, change has always been a challenge to humankind. History shows countless examples of resistance to change. The first successful cast iron plough, invented in the United States in 1797, was rejected by New Jersey farmers due to the theory that cast iron poisoned the land and stimulated the growth of weeds.

Henry Ford was considered a radical with no business instincts, but he managed to manufacture a reliable car costing no more than a horse and buggy. Those who loaned Robert Fulton money for his steamboat project stipulated that their names be withheld, for fear of ridicule were it known they supported anything so foolhardy. In 1976 Jobs and Wozniak tried to sell the Apple computer concept to Commodore Computers for $100 000. Commodore refused the offer, as did Atari and Hewlett-Packard, not believing that there was a future in personal computers.

Initial market tests showed that consumers would not buy Swatch watches because they were too unusual. It was the same with jogging shoes. Sporting goods companies repeatedly turned down the proposition to produce jogging shoes, telling the originators of NIKE to stick to their own expertise and stop telling them how to produce what they knew best: shoes.

These stories are amusing in retrospect but remain amazing examples of resistance to change. Many people feel resistance to change in everyday life. Our reaction to conditioning is part of what we perceive as the threat of change, and the following diagram is designed to give you options to take you from the threat or the resistance to change, to the choices created by recognising opportunity. Try these choices when you are challenged by change.

Challenge your mind

THREAT	OPPORTUNITY
Conditioning	⮕ Expand horizons of thinking – look outside the square
Criticism	⮕ Learn new ways of doing things
Stay with what you know	⮕ Expand your goals
Comfort zones	⮕ Take a risk, get out of your safety zones
Fear	⮕ Do something you are afraid of
Resentment or blame	⮕ Let go of the past and see change as an opportunity to grow
Negative judgement	⮕ Accept people as they are and create opportunities for them

Change can come in many forms and can throw you way out of your comfort zone; often we don't embrace change because we fear the outcome. I worked with a large government organisation that commissioned me to run a series of talks about how to handle change. The organisation was decentralising and changing its culture to be based on reward for performance, rather than reward for how long a person had been with the organisation. Very big changes were afoot and about 90 per cent of the group was in fear; fear of what lay ahead, of not knowing whether they could deal with the changes that lay ahead.

Take a risk, get out of your comfort zone

~~~~~~~

Many employees feared losing the job security they had taken for granted for so long. Some wondered whether they would have enough skills for the future organisation. One particular fellow, Edward – I remember him clearly – was terrified that he would have to move desks. He had had the same desk for the last 20 years, on the same floor, in the same building. He had never encouraged an environment for change for himself, and he was paying dearly for it during this time of turmoil.

Others feared rejection, rejection by their peers for not being able to keep up with new or differing guidelines. Edina feared ridicule; she was a very shy woman in her 40s who had come straight from school into the government organisation as a girl of 15 and had never known anything else. The last thing she wanted was someone ridiculing her for not being able to keep up with the new rules.

Fear of failure kept these people in a cycle in which they perceived change as a threat, rather than as an opportunity for them to learn to grow and to expand their skills. Those who chose to move forward did so and became more valuable to the organisation as a result. Some took a 'package', a sum of money and an early retirement. But there was a band of about 15 per cent in the organisation who remained and became enormously resentful because those in it couldn't have their way. They became resistant to any new thoughts or ideas or systems and as a result became revengeful. The only problem with revenge is that it hurts the person feeling it a whole lot more than it hurts the person one is feeling it about. Eventually the need for everyone to perform in the organisation overcame them and this group of *dinosaurs* mostly disappeared, in much the same way as the original dinosaur did millions of years ago.

What can I do about this that is positive?

~~~~

Of course, there is some change that is not positive, like the death of someone you really love, or the unnecessary hurting of another human being, things that seem senseless and random. When things go wrong, think, 'What can I do about this that is positive?' and if there is truly nothing, eventually you have to accept it and move on. You'll be surprised though, how, in retrospect, even the worse possible situation can become a learning point in your life. A positive attitude toward life is one that takes the whole view of experiences. The wise person sees problems as challenges, and values them for the lessons that they offer. In this way, all experiences eventually become good.

We must stop teaching that

opportunity knocks. It never knocks.

You can listen at the door for ten lifetimes,

but you won't hear it knocking.

You are opportunity. You open the door.

MAXWELL MALTZ, M.D.

When you are at the point of seeing a change as bad, ask yourself:

How do I feel?
How do I want to feel?
Is what I am doing helping me to feel good?
Why am I doing this?
How do I get the feeling that I desire?

Everyone has a different way of dealing with change, and different timings. The four basic ways we change our minds when we get new and conflicting information are:

◆ *Change by exception*, where our old belief system remains intact but allows for a handful of anomalies. For instance, a person who dislikes all members of a particular group except one or two. Or a person who considers psychic phenomena nonsense, yet still believes that their great aunt's dreams came true. These are dismissed as 'the exceptions that prove the rule' instead of the exceptions that disprove the rule.

◆ *Incremental change*, which occurs bit by bit, and the individual is not aware of having changed.

◆ *Pendulum change*, the abandonment of one closed and certain system for another. For example, a hawk becomes a dove; the disenchanted religious zealot becomes an atheist; the promiscuous person becomes a prude. Pendulum change is where the person rejects their own prior experience, going from one kind of half-knowing to another.

◆ *Paradigm change*, which is the fourth dimension of change, the insight that allows all information to come together in a new form or structure. It is the most challenging kind of change because it relinquishes certainty. It allows for different interpretations from different perspectives at different times.

97

Change by exception says, 'I'm right, except for...' Incremental change says, 'I was almost right, but now I'm right.' Pendulum change says, 'I was wrong before, but now I'm right.' Paradigm change says, 'I was partially right before, and now I'm a bit more partially right.'

In paradigm change we realise that our previous views were only part of the picture – and that what we know now is only part of what we'll know later. Change, then, is no longer threatening. It absorbs, enlarges, enriches. The unknown becomes interesting territory. Each insight widens the road, making the next stage of travel, the next opening, easier.

Choose paradigm change

Change itself changes, just as in nature evolution grows from a simple to a complex process. Every new occurrence alters the nature of those to follow. Paradigm change is not a simple linear effect, like the 10 little Indians in the nursery rhyme who vanish one by one. It is a sudden shift of pattern, a spiral, and sometimes a cataclysm.

Don't be afraid of change; it signifies the entry into something new. Your anxiety is just letting you know that you are leaving your safety zone. Be gentle on yourself while you are experiencing change, trusting that you have made the right decision. I find that whenever I want to 'fast forward' an experience, that's when I learn the most. Whenever I wish for a problem to go away, and feel that I can't bear it a minute more, I know in my heart that is when I'm developing valuable coping skills for the future.

Continually revise and set new goals in your life and accept that change is a part of setting those goals. The time, the energy and the commitment that you give those goals will then show itself in your life, your style and your attitude.

Be gentle on yourself

~~~

The only thing that is certain for man is change.

LEO BUSCAGLIA

How to Use Change as a Positive

☑ Desire creates the power for change

☑ Recognise change as an opportunity

☑ Be proactive about change

☑ Just because you have always done it this way doesn't make it the most appropriate way now

☑ Challenge your mind

☑ Take a risk, get out of your comfort zone

☑ What can I do about this that is positive?

☑ Choose paradigm change

☑ Be gentle on yourself

THE **5** KEY

Presentation

---

*Matching the Book
with the Cover*

THE VEHICLE

Matching Self Image
with Self Esteem

Elizabeth's story

Elizabeth was growing up, but she was also growing out. She had found that the mirror was reflecting an image of herself that she didn't like; in fact, she weighed herself and found she had gained two stone (12 kilograms) in weight. She knew she had been eating more than usual lately, and what she was eating was largely junk food. But there was more to it than that; she had somehow slipped back into being negative about herself. Insecurity had struck with a vengeance.

Peer pressure was omnipresent. The girls she mixed with seemed to talk of almost nothing else apart from their appearance, and especially their size and their weight. The way they talked about it disturbed her; it was as if such things were all that mattered on earth. Relationships didn't matter, study didn't matter, almost nothing else mattered to them except their size.

Somehow Elizabeth had got sucked into the vortex of self obsession. She realised this and was pleased she had, because now she could do something about it. She knew about visualisation and had had such success with it that she decided to adapt the idea a little and use it to help her to change her attitude and her appearance. She began by seeing herself in her mind's eye as happy, as a person who was full of joy. This was very difficult at first because it really wasn't the way she felt, but, bit by bit, she extended the period of time that she could think of herself as being happy and joyous.

She found a way for nature to help her. She would sit in her garden alone and observe the trees or the sky, or just a blade of grass. She would give her whole attention to it and, while observing its beauty, she would become completely absorbed in the loveliness of it. She could see the light reflecting off it and the colours that seemed to

envelop it. As she sat in the stillness of nature, she would lose track of time.

After 10 minutes or half an hour, she would always feel refreshed and energised, tingling as if she had just had a cold shower. Because this made her feel great, she set aside part of every day to spend time observing in the garden. She also took the feeling of safeness and serenity back into the house with her, and her brothers and sisters noticed how content and happy she appeared to be. This seemed to have a calming effect on them as well; in fact, it had a positive effect on the whole household.

Elizabeth changed the type of food she was eating to give herself a more balanced diet: grain with vegetables and fruit and a little bit of protein every day. She didn't seem to crave the junk food she had longed for before. She had tricked herself, or so she described it. When she looked into the mirror she would see herself at her very best, straight and tall and slim. When she looked into the mirror long enough, out of the corner of her eye she could really see this new image.

It took six months for Elizabeth's body to catch up with the image she saw in the mirror: the image of a lovely young woman. When she did, it was if she had always been that way. But she never forgot to visit her garden every day, and even if there was no garden where she was, she could still visit the garden in her imagination.

Elizabeth's story

Like attracts like.
Whatever the conscious mind
thinks and believes,
the subconscious identically creates.

BRIAN ADAMS

Matching Self Image
with Self Esteem

We care a great deal about what people think of us. We've invented fashion, advertising and the media. Individuals and companies spend large amounts of money creating the images they desire in the marketplace; while there may be a few individuals strong enough or wealthy enough not to care what the world thinks of them, most care a great deal. Being accepted and loved by others is an unspoken goal that most people possess, whether they are prepared to acknowledge it or not.

The key is to match your external image, or presentation, with your self esteem, or self value. Many people just judge the cover of a person, despite the fact that experience tells them that they may be totally wrong. By judging someone negatively on first sight, you can dismiss great opportunities for learning, for growth and for understanding. You rely on image to give you feedback about others all the time. Your eyes give you instant information, whether real or imagined, true or false.

Our verbal messages, or the words we use, account for 7 per cent of what is believed by others. Our vocal messages, the way we say it, account for 36 per cent of what is believed by others. Our visual messages, what others see, account for 57 per cent of what is believed by others. So visual presentation has a very strong impact. Everything you wear makes a statement about you. The legal fraternity spends thousands of dollars on black robes and white horse-hair wigs, not because they are particularly comfortable but because they make a statement about the wearer, a statement that what they are doing matches how they present themselves.

People expect others to look the part. A professional appearance is taken as a reflection of attitude. The person who looks smart, successful and professional usually is. I'm not suggesting you race out and spend a small fortune on expensive clothes and accessories, but you have to invest in the appropriate clothes before you can become what the clothes represent. I've known men and women to have one or two basic outfits and by using these creatively, they manage to look professional and stylish every day of the week. It doesn't matter whether your job is glamorous, or behind the scenes, or whether it is cleaning and tidying, the way you present yourself has an enormous impact.

Appearance means so much, because first impressions sometimes stick. The aspects we use to size up others on the first meeting are: skin colour, gender, age, general appearance, eyes, facial expression (your smile has the highest impact), personal space, movement, touch and smell.

First impressions have a high impact

Very often you can't get past first base with a person and you can't understand why. Almost always it's because you have been sized up by them in the first couple of minutes, and have been found wanting. They have found something about your appearance or your body language that they don't like and their decision has been made. You can talk yourself blue in the face, but they might well never change that very first opinion of you.

It may not be anything big or important. It could be a scuffed shoe, or chipped or dirty fingernails. It may be defensive body language, or offensive body odour. Although, as the old saying goes, 'You cannot judge a book by its cover', people will certainly try to. It is not good, but it is reality, so you need to be aware of the impact your cover has on others.

Match your image with what you want to say about yourself

The marketplace will get confused if what you're saying doesn't match the way you look. Suppose you've spent days preparing an articulate, well thought out presentation for a job interview, you've had your CV neatly bound, a work of art. If you then slouch in wearing casual clothes and toss the CV onto the table, the person or people you're presenting yourself to will be totally confused. How you present the information about yourself will influence the way you are judged by people. Be aware of what the people you are presenting to are thinking and help them make a favourable assessment of you by dressing for the occasion.

When you go to a party or a social engagement, you either dress for comfort, for the occasion, or to impress – even if you decide to dress down. You create the appropriate external appearance to match your self image, but true self image goes a lot deeper.

You are special and unique

The story of Captain Bligh of *HMS Bounty* is an extraordinary example of a man keeping a strong image of survival and the self esteem of his crew on a positive footing. In the midst of enormous challenges, he focused on the image and matched his behaviour and that of his crew to this image. Captain Bligh has been much maligned in history; few people understand that he was one of the most exceptional men ever to command a King's Ship.

He became Captain after working his way up through the ranks, the first time anyone had achieved this in the Royal Navy. The *Bounty* was his first command, with a crew made up of convicts from the prison hulks of London.

When this disorganised, motley crew, led by the third mate, Fletcher Christian, commandeered the *Bounty* and set Bligh and 22 others adrift in a small open boat, Captain Bligh responded like the true believer in his survival that he was.

As the *Bounty* sailed away, leaving them to almost certain death, Bligh spoke to each of the 22 men in the small boat. He took them by the hand, one by one, and asked for a pledge of loyalty, trust and acceptance. He then asked them to see themselves landing safely on home territory, to believe it in their minds. Thus began his commitment to building his team's self esteem for the hard journey home.

Bligh then charted a course for the nearest port, which happened to be over 3500 miles (5600 kilometres) away. The journey was, by all standards, totally impossible. The boat was too small. There wasn't enough food or water.

But Captain Bligh and his crew made it. They lost one man, speared by natives, and they suffered terribly from heat and thirst. But by studying the wind and the sea, Bligh found small islands to stop at for food and fresh water. He made charts of the seas through which they sailed; he was confident and he made his men feel confident. What is the point of keeping a record if the boat and its crew are doomed to failure? Bligh refused to accept failure. He refused to give up the vision of his survival and he motivated his crew to expect that same vision. He lashed himself to the tiller, as if to say, 'Here I am and here I stay. We're in this together.'

It was an epic journey from the South Pacific across to the Dutch East Indies. Bligh and his crew made it to safety – with their clothes in tatters and all but Bligh himself unconscious in the bottom of the boat. But when they arrived at the dock, Bligh refused to leave his boat. He sent a child on the dockside to fetch the governor of the port, and when he arrived, Captain Bligh staggered to his feet and saluted. His words were, 'Permission to come ashore, Sir?' just as he had seen it in his imagination.

Captain Bligh had a strong vision of survival. He matched this with his self image, then invested time and energy into matching his and his crew's self esteem to that vision and self image.

Self image is how you see yourself; and this image is lodged in your subconscious. The major purpose of your subconscious is to achieve your image of yourself, so it matters a great deal what that image is. You give instructions to your self image through your self talk and self imaging; so do be careful what you talk about.

A friend told me recently that she had to give up a relationship with a long-time friend and said how hard that decision was. She and Bea had been friends for 20 years but as they grew older, Bea became cynical and picky about her and their mutual friends. Every comment that came out of Bea's mouth seemed to be a put down about someone or something.

My friend noticed that whenever she was with Bea her energy was low and she felt an unusually high degree of anxiety. Her self talk always became more negative after she was with Bea, and she decided that although she loved Bea a great deal, she didn't like her. She had to make the tough decision not to see her any more, and they drifted apart.

You become what you think about and, for her self survival, my friend had to let go of her friendship with Bea.

Your self image is constantly being modified in accordance with your environment as you experience it. From these experiences you develop a set of labels to attach to yourself that summarise your inner picture and expectations. These describe the basic beliefs that guide your behaviour.

It is impossible to be any better than your own self image

You have a clear image of yourself and, whether you acknowledge this or not, how you see yourself determines who you are; it is impossible to exceed your current self image. So if you wish to change or improve something, first of all you will need to change the picture you have of yourself.

The battle to change what we are begins with self image. Maxwell Maltz, in his book *Psycho-Cybernetics*, discusses how, as a plastic surgeon, he reconstructed people's exterior images exactly as they wanted them to be, but a large proportion still thought they were unattractive because they would not accept the new external image. They believed no one had altered their image.

Dr Maltz was astounded with the number of people who he had helped to create new faces and new bodies who would not accept their new image, saying they were still 'ugly' or 'unattractive'. He decided to get out of plastic surgery and work in the area of psycho-cybernetics, the science of the mind, because he felt that if he could help people accept themselves by changing their self image, having cosmetic surgery might not even be necessary.

Like your self image

Liking your self image is an essential part of successful living. Young women who become obsessed with their weight, body shape and size have not come to terms with their self image. They give themselves a very hard time about some ideal that belongs in a fashion magazine, rather than liking and accepting who they are and getting on with their life. People who are anorexic refuse to see the image in the mirror in front of them. Their picture of themselves is so different from reality. They refuse to accept what they see and are compulsive about becoming what they think should be their perfect weight.

I talked with a married couple who went on a diet to change their self image. Jim and Betty decided the exact weight and the exact shape they were aiming for, and they were successful, staying on the food that was suggested by the Weight Watchers group that they had joined. After the first three months they were on their maintenance program. They both stuck to this religiously except for one meal a day. That was lunch, and it was Jim that used to have the occasional 'pig-out', not Betty. So it was a great surprise when, after another three months, Betty was gaining weight, eventually returning to the original size she had been before her weight loss.

When I talked with them, the only difference was in their thinking. Betty could not change the image she had of herself in her mind; she had always seen herself as a bit chubby and could not believe that she could be anything else. Jim, on the other hand, believed he could be slimmer without a doubt, and was able to sustain his desired weight. Betty's story is not uncommon; the challenge for her was in going for a change in attitude that would match her changed appearance.

Change your image in your head first

The most successful method of achieving this new *visual image* is to use visualisation as a tool.

Self image exercise

Close your eyes, relax your body and imagine you are in a beautiful garden. See yourself sitting on a big, comfortable garden bench. Imagine all the beautiful trees and flowers around you. As this is your own creation, you can make it as beautiful as you wish it to be. Make the colours bold and exquisitely beautiful. Make the yellows clean and clear. Make the sky the softest blue. See the trees tall and straight. Hear the birds singing the sweetest melody. Smell the freshness of the grass, the delicate scent of the flowers. Let your imagination run wild.

Imagine, as you are sitting on this garden bench, that you can see someone walking toward you. You can't make out who it is because they are too far away, but as they come closer, you can see that this person looks just like you. In fact, as you watch, you realise that it is you. The only difference is that you are looking at your absolute best. Your face is happy and relaxed; your eyes are shining with inner wisdom. You are standing straight and tall, and you are your ideal weight. Everything that you have ever thought you would like to be is in this mirror image as it comes toward you and sits silently beside you on the garden bench.

Imagine that your mirror image sits so close to you that you and that image merge. Imagine that you become this lovely person, your projected image. While you are imagining this, think of how it would make you feel to be like this. Imagine how you would sit, how you would move, how you would think and talk, imagine how you would be. Hold that feeling for as long as you can.

When you are ready, open your eyes, still holding on to that image, and take this image with you in your mind wherever you go.

Suspend old memories

You change your self image by suspending the old memories, while you present a new set of more desirable images to the subconscious through visualisation. If you do this often enough and vividly enough, the old memories will eventually be obscured by your more recent visualisation. Your new images will be absorbed quickly when you are relaxed enough to stop the presentation of a lifetime of old images to the brain.

The subconscious can't tell fact from fiction, reality from illusion; it has no moral judgment. All it can do is go for what is vividly imagined through self image and self talk. This self talk is strongly influenced by the people you encounter and the experiences you have every day. So if your dominant thought is to achieve a specific goal or to have a particular kind of relationship with someone, then your subconscious will be working towards that goal. Mental rehearsal, called visualisation, has an enormously strong impact on what you achieve. So it's important that your dominant goal (or thought) is something you desire, rather than something you are afraid of, because the subconscious will drive forward to get that just as enthusiastically.

We cannot move away from that which we do not want. We can only move toward what it is we do want. For instance, your goal for improving a performance level at work needs to be active: 'I will read and apply the new data to my work', not 'I don't want to make any mistakes with the new data'. We cannot achieve a goal that is in the negative. 'Don't forget to bring the milk home' is a classic example. All the subconscious mind hears is: 'Forget to bring home the milk'; it does not take in 'Don't'. So in asking your partner to bring home the milk, create a visual picture for him or her to follow, such as: 'Honey, I am making your favourite banana custard tonight with shaved cinnamon on top. Could you please bring home some milk for this?'

When sending the children out to school, you need to say, 'Please look to the right and left before crossing the road', not 'Don't get run over'. Creating a visual picture for safety is essential.

Positive mental images enhance performance

It is what we are moving towards that makes the difference, not what we are moving away from. Positive mental images enhance performance. High achievers and people high on self efficacy have positive mental images. Their future is decided more by how they think rather than what they know. In the end, it is what they do with what they know that really counts.

Once the image is securely lodged in the subconscious mind, the next step is to match it with your self esteem, or your self value. Where self image is a mind process, self esteem is a feeling. It's a sense of confidence and compe-tence, trusting yourself and trusting that you will always be able to deal with what comes your way.

Know the purpose we seek if life, for then,
like archers aiming at a definite mark, we shall
be more likely to attain what we want.

ARISTOTLE

113

You will always be enough for any situation

Self esteem is the feeling that you will always be able to produce desirable outcomes, whatever they may be. It is approving of yourself, unconditionally liking yourself no matter what the evidence may show at the time. It is being able to hold on to the belief that your essential nature is good and believing this through the hard times as well as the good. It is knowing that you deserve pleasure and having the willingness and the capacity to create it and accept it frequently.

Being able to make time for yourself every day does wonderful things for your self esteem. Take the time out to do something for yourself that you really enjoy, relaxing in whatever way makes you happy, something that is away from work, family and commitments.

Self esteem is the ability to laugh at yourself, not to take yourself too seriously and to allow yourself some fun. It is the willingness to be foolish.

Drop your facade and allow your real self to be exposed

The willingness to be light-hearted will allow you to drop your facade and let people experience the real you. Often people are so busy trying to be someone that they think everyone else will like, they don't let their real self (which is usually perfect as it is) be shown. They end up pleasing no one.

Self esteem is also allowing others to be who they are, to accept them unconditionally. If you have the courage to accept others for what they are, life will be much easier. If what they are is not your cup of tea, fine, you don't have to spend time with them. You don't have to like everyone you meet, but since you haven't walked in their shoes, you have no right to judge them.

Listen to the coincidences

～～～

Everyone has intuition. You are born with it; whether you choose to use it or not is your choice. However, if intuition has not been used for a period of time, it may need to be coached back into working order.

Coincidences occur around you all the time. You want some information, and the morning paper has an article on the very subject, just when you needed it. You want to speak with a person that you have been thinking about, and the phone rings and it is them, right out of the blue. You have no money left to draw on, you have no idea where you will get it from and someone repays a loan you had forgotten about, or you find $100 that you had forgotten about in a sock in your bottom drawer.

Although coincidences occur all the time, some are not so obvious, so you will need to be alert to recognise them. They sometimes come in the form of intuition, so if you get a very strong feeling to do something or not to do something, listen to it; it is your intuition speaking to you.

To get this working more effectively in your life, all you have to do is to honour it, to trust it, and to use it. People who have the ability to trust their intuition usually have high self esteem because they are trusting their wisdom and their intuition collectively.

The sky knows the reason and the patterns behind the clouds, and you will know, too, when you lift yourself high enough to see beyond horizons.

RICHARD BACH

How to develop self esteem

~~~~~~

Self esteem or self value, like coincidence, needs to be acknowledged and built on regularly. Here are some ways to develop good self value.

◆ *When you cook just for yourself, make your favourite dish and serve it on the best crockery, with the best silver, and pour your favourite drink into the best glass you have; set the table as if you were the guest of honour and then enjoy every bit of it.*

◆ *Take yourself on a holiday, somewhere you have always wanted to go; it doesn't have to be expensive, but if it is and you have the money, all the better.*

◆ *Go first class, give yourself the best quality.*

◆ *Talk to yourself as if you were your own best friend.*

◆ *Make your work or home area your specific environment, absolutely yours, by personalising it with your special things that say who you are and what you stand for.*

◆ *Breathe deeply often (deep diaphragm breathing); it centres you and gives you a burst of oxygen which benefits the whole body.*

◆ *Have a really great photo or portrait taken of you and have it in your home; see yourself in your best possible light.*

◆ *Play your favourite music in your car, as loudly as you want.*

◆ *Give yourself the best posture you can, stretch regularly (like a cat); stand tall and straight.*

◆ *Pat yourself on the back for all your achievements; whether they are big or small, they are all as important as each other.*

◆ *Be kind to yourself when you make mistakes or get off the track.*

◆ *Learn quickly and then move on to new and more exciting challenges.*

◆ *Speak kindly to yourself and to others, your subconscious is always listening.*

There is a difference between self esteem and perfectionism. With self esteem, you accept and work with what you have, respecting where you have come from and who you are now. Then, if you want, you change this through your self image. Perfectionism, on the other hand, is based on a painful illusion, the illusion of personal perfectibility, people measuring themselves against impossible standards. Perfectionists lose sight of the quality of life in their search for an ideal. They can only see perfect or imperfect, so they are unable to enjoy any activity or person in between.

Sometimes they give up and become total failures. Some just feel inadequate, but try to conceal it by demanding perfection from others, or procrastinate, afraid of making mistakes.

Perfectionism is an illusion

With perfectionism, as soon as you reach the desired state, the desired state moves on, so it is impossible to gain perfection. It is an illusion. Don't confuse it with excellence. If you are a perfectionist, relax, enjoy life, put as much effort into doing something just for the experience, not for how it is going to turn out. Become less critical and enjoy life, instead of controlling it.

Perfectionists can become obsessive in their behaviour. Maisy, a self-confessed perfectionist had to have all her clothes hanging in a 'perfect' row in her closet. She was a normal person except for her drive for everything being 'just so'. This perfectionism began to extend into her life in other ways too. She would get frustrated about family gatherings or outings that didn't meet her ideal of perfection. She would criticise everyone else for what she saw to be wrong about them, for not doing whatever she wanted, so that they never met with her approval. She said that the gatherings were never held at the right places or at the right time of day, or that none of the right people had been invited.

Eventually, Maisy stopped being asked out on outings. It was impossible to be with her, nothing was ever enough, or the right shape, or size, or at the right time. But it was herself whom she was driving crazy the most.

Success is the quality of your journey

Perfectionists can never reach their ideal; they are doomed even before they begin their journey. Success is the quality of the journey, not the destination, and perfectionists emphasise the end result rather than the journey.

I remember standing in the kitchen organising the children for a Sunday picnic. I was tense, uptight, trying to stop their fighting and squabbling. I was packing the picnic hamper and feeling as tight as a tightrope. My voice was at a high pitch and I was out of control.

All of a sudden, it struck me that I was planning for the 'perfect' outing, and was seeing this vision in my head. But what kind of mental state would I be in to enjoy this 'perfect' picnic if my stress levels kept rising this way. I realised that getting ready for the picnic, packing the basket, helping the children get dressed and ready was just as important as the actual picnic. I laughed, let go of my stress and enjoyed the journey to the picnic just as much as actually getting there.

Let go of perfectionism so that your self esteem, your self value, may rise to the surface. Match that self esteem with a clear self image, a self image that reflects who you really are and where you are going.

Be willing to see yourself as the cause of the condition and circumstances of your life. See it as a mark of exceptionally high self esteem. Accept responsibility for your life, warts and all. The ability to do this frees you to go on to the next step, but if you are still blaming everyone for the woes of your existence, it is almost impossible to move on. Wherever you are, love yourself for getting you there, then move on, as quickly or as slowly as you like, but move on.

Accept responsibility for what you have created

~~~~~~

Where there is love there is life.

MOHANDAS GANDHI

Matching Self Image with Self Esteem

☑ First impressions have a high impact

☑ Match your image with what you want to say
about yourself

☑ You are special and unique

☑ It is impossible to be any better than your own self image

☑ Like your self image

☑ Change your image in your head first

☑ Suspend old memories

☑ Positive mental images enhance performance

☑ You will always be enough for any situation

☑ Drop your facade and allow your real self to be exposed

☑ Listen to the coincidences

☑ How to develop self esteem

☑ Perfectionism is an illusion

☑ Success is the quality of your journey

☑ Accept responsibility for what you have created

Forgive Quickly

You Will Eventually,
So Why Not Now?

THE VEHICLE

Opening Your Heart

Elizabeth's story

Yet another invitation to the seaside arrived at Elizabeth's house for the Easter vacation. Her friend from school wanted her to visit. Elizabeth was stubborn; she was mad at Eve, mad because Eve didn't make the effort to come to her mother's funeral so long ago. At the time, she couldn't understand it. Eve and Elizabeth's Mum had been close; Eve always listened to her and seemed to have a close bond with her.

Eve didn't tell Elizabeth at the time, but the reason she couldn't bring herself to go to the funeral was because she had this feeling that she wanted to remember Elizabeth's mother happily, with love and joy not sorrow and grief. She felt that her friend's mother was still around for her. At least she existed in her thoughts and she was protective of keeping this image of her just as it was.

Years later it still made Elizabeth angry that Eve could let her down at a time like that. So, subconsciously, she punished Eve, punished her for not doing something she had wanted her to do. It had been years since they had seen each other.

Elizabeth missed Eve's friendship enormously – the face-to-face stuff, talking till the early hours about all the things that were important to them, the feeling that no matter how long they hadn't seen each other, it was as if the other had just been out to buy the papers and come back.

Elizabeth really wanted to see Eve. But she also wanted to take a stand about her not coming to her Mum's funeral and to feel bitterness and resentment over it, even though she had never asked Eve why or what had happened to make her choose not to be there. She had to go deep inside herself to find her heart and rekindle the love between herself and Eve, to forgive Eve for what she thought Eve had done to her.

In the end Elizabeth decided to go for the goal, which was to love and be loved by Eve, rather than being right or, more to the point, righteous.

Elizabeth let go of her resentment and joined her friend at the seaside. After they were together for five minutes, sitting on the beach laughing out loud, Elizabeth could not remember what all the fuss had been about, how badly she had felt for those years. The joy of being with her best friend far outweighed all the bitterness she had felt before.

She had to access this through her heart and learn that when she closed her heart, it was she who hurt the most as a result. So she forgave herself and forgave Eve and opened her heart to life's experiences again.

Elizabeth's story

We win by tenderness,
we conquer by forgiveness.

FREDRICK WILLIAM ROBERTSON

Open Your Heart

When you open your heart to others, there is always a risk involved. You could get hurt, you could become resentful because the outcome didn't go the way you desired. You have many choices about how to respond, how to receive and how to transmit.

One of the biggest choices you have is how and when to forgive. Forgiving is just as much about forgiving yourself as about forgiving others. You have an enormous capacity to forgive. Time does heal all wounds, and forgiving heals wounds even quicker.

Let go of old resentments

So many people have resentments about people or events in their life. They resent not having enough education, or too much; not enough love, or too much. They resent something that happened when they were 10 years old. You wouldn't be human unless you had some resentment from the past. The key is to realise what you learnt from the experience, accept it as a point of gaining wisdom and insight, then stop focusing on being badly done by; accept the wisdom gained, let go and move on.

When you lock into resentment, resistance occurs, resistance to what you could learn from having felt that resentment in the first place. Whenever you resent something that has happened, it is usually because it has (a) hit a raw nerve, (b) been true, (c) been untrue, (d) been unfair. If you can ascertain which one of these applies to your resentment, then you can start taking 50 per cent responsibility for creating the problem in the first place and get on to what you can learn from the experience.

Those who cannot move out of resentment and resistance will find themselves automatically locking into revenge, trying to get even. Revenge is sometimes very obvious, like someone who won't talk to a particular person to punish them. Sometimes it is subtle; they smile on the outside but behind their backs they say negative, put-down things about that person. I've seen revenge take its toll in companies where one employee felt revenge for the company and decided to single-handedly bring it down.

Revenge can be physical, one person hurts another, then the other hurts that person back. I've never understood how that makes it right or better. Now there are two of them doing it instead of one. Physical abuse rarely solves the original problem.

An unforgiving mind has its own agenda.
It includes distorting what is real
until it is barely recognisable.

G. JAMPOLSKY

Revenge rarely satisfies

~~~

If you get into the cycle of feeling revenge, then resisting the learning experience, then wasting more time feeling revenge, this cycle is often very difficult to break.

Focus on the opportunity to learn, rather than the revenge. Focusing on revenge may give you a flutter of righteousness some time down the track, but

To forgive is the highest, most beautiful form of love. In return, you will receive untold peace and happiness.

ROBERT MULLER

it rarely gives you any pleasure in the meantime, because, in the meantime, resentments are often used to *beat yourself up* over what did, or didn't happen.

Polly was part of a company restructure, except she got restructured out of the company altogether. She was angry and hurt, but mostly resentful. She decided to get even; she did something to that company that cost them tens of thousands of dollars. She thought she had got even, but she was never the same after doing what she had done. The guilt nearly tore her in two. She lost her nerve for work, her energy, and she became unemployable. She created her worst nightmare instead of using her resentment as a learning experience and making herself stronger. She got even and devalued herself.

Polly took her resentment and turned it against herself. We all have resentments, they are a natural part of life; they become unnatural when we begin to dwell on them, rather than seeing them in perspective with the rest of our lives.

Some resentments begin in the schoolyard. You may start out with no resentments in life, but the schoolyard can be a breeding ground for them. Children verbally or physically hurt others because they are different, whatever those differences are: colour, race, height, sex, economics, or even what food a child takes in their lunchbox. Some lifelong resentments that relate to other cultures can start from small incidents so long ago. A man I know, Ivan, hates a particular race of people, all because of a punch-up that happened in the playground with another boy his age who was from a different country, and for his entire life he has gone on hating the whole race as a result of that particular incident.

Imagine you have an empty sack. Wherever you go or whatever you do, you carry the sack with you. The sack is for your resentments. As you grow up, you experience disappointments and let-downs, like rejection from a girlfriend or boyfriend, or being badly treated by a teacher. In they go, filling that sack. Some people will experience a job loss during their working life, and will feel the bitter disappointment attached to that. Some will feel the disappointment and resentment of a divorce; whether you are one of the partners or part of the family, the pain is just as acute.

All of these things are part of life, part of the learning experience. Don't get down-and-out. If you bring out all your resentments and wallow in them, then there can be no individual growth or development. Try this visualisation exercise to let go of those old resentments that are holding you back.

Visualisation exercise

Imagine you have a sack full of resentments from the past: unresolved grievances, unhappy feelings about a situation or person, pent-up emotion about a person that has gone unexpressed.

I want you to take that sack over to a comfortable chair, sit down, open it up, spill all the resentments out onto the carpet and then wallow in them. Have a great time, complain, feel sad, feel badly done by, feel upset, feel out of control. Feel them all thoroughly, for one minute.

Now, collect all these feelings, pick them all up from the floor, and wrap them up into a bundle. Lift the sack up and take it over to an imaginary window, open the window, then throw the sack out as far as you can. Wonderful.

Shut the imaginary window tight, and leave all the negative feelings about the past behind you. They have served you well in the past and now they are finished with, over, past their use by date.

Now focus on all the wonderful things you wish to create in the future. See yourself achieving all the goals you desire, all the abundance you wish. See yourself creating this in living colour. Sit and dream for a moment, and when you are ready, open your eyes and feel the feeling of abundance all around you, the feeling of fulfilment, joy, fullness and beauty all around you.

Learn from mistakes

~~~~~

It is hard to learn to forgive yourself, especially when you have made a mistake, and yet that's how you learn. Henry Ford senior understood about mistakes; he only promoted people in his automotive company who made them. His theory was that if people weren't prepared to risk mistakes, they would not have radical insight or make discoveries in the automotive industry, so what value were they to him?

He rewarded people for trying, by saying, 'If you make mistakes, great, learn from them and move on.' As long as they were moving forward in the development of producing the best quality motor car, he didn't care how many mistakes his people made.

The electric light bulb was discovered after 1000 mistakes. Dunlop discovered the key to producing rubber after throwing his invention into a fire. In his anger at the countless mistakes he'd made, he discovered that adding heat was the missing process in producing rubber successfully.

Relationships are a wonderful learning ground

~~~~~

Jeanie's story brings home how relationships help us to learn and move on. She and I were close friends when we were 15 years old. She meet Dan at a birthday party. I was there; I watched her fall in love. She fell madly in love, but Dan was an aloof young man who stood away from life; he was a watcher rather than a player.

Dan fell in love also, but his passion was expressed in very different ways. He demonstrated his affection by criticising her, by evaluating her. It was his way. Jeanie simply loved him, sent him love letters, brought him love songs;

the more she showed him her affection, the more critical he became. When they broke up, she took it very much to heart, while he just drifted off, seeming not to care.

Twenty-five years passed, then, out of the blue, Dan got in contact with Jeanie through her parents, who lived at the same house as they had when she was fifteen. Jeanie was surprised that Dan wanted to meet with her; it seemed out of character for the Dan she had known so long ago.

When they met, he was warm, friendly, talkative, interesting and interested. They talked vivaciously, laughed, remembered and had fun. Their lives had been full; they both had experienced joy and heartache. They sat talking as if time had stood still, and he told her how important she had been in his life, how, as his first girlfriend, she had given him confidence, happiness and love, and he said how much that meant to him in his life.

When she told me of her reunion, she said this: 'I am so pleased that I didn't walk away from that relationship bitter or resentful; because I would have been wrong. I'm so very glad that I chose to learn from Dan, so long ago.'

It took Jeanie 25 years to find out that Dan was not a mistake. Sometimes we never find out. It doesn't matter.

There are people looking for exactly
what you have to offer, and
you are being brought together
on the checker board of life.

LOUISE L. HAY

When you make mistakes, that's when you need self acceptance the most

Being human, you will often not do the 'right' thing and often say the 'wrong' thing. It is easy to lose focus when you are trying to do the 'right' thing for everyone else. This is a normal part of learning, and it is when you lose focus that you need to be gentle on yourself the most. This is when you need love and nurturing the most, not to give yourself a mental beating. You need to open your heart, to let go of old hurts and to love yourself for who and what you are right now.

When I see someone being unkind or hurtful to another person, I sense that comes from being unhappy or sad or resentful. I know that the person being unkind is treating themselves even more unkindly. That person's self talk is more negative than positive. The extension of someone being hard on themselves is to be unreasonably hard on others.

If only you could see your faults as being as valuable as every other part of you. Your inadequacies are your learning points. Be gentle on yourself and others while you are learning; nurture yourself. Acknowledge that this is a learning phase and be kind to yourself through your self talk. Take good physical care of yourself and your environment. Make things pleasant around you while you are learning.

Whatever you are doing
love yourself for doing it.

THADDEUS GOLAS

Life is about starts and finishes

~~~~~~

Life is about starts and finishes, how quickly you can learn, love, let go, forgive, leave behind the past, live in the present and create your future. If you get stuck in the same sickness, bitterness or guilt of last year or the year before that, with resentment, hate, guilt or jealousy clogging you up, then it is impossible for you to set a clear, clean goal for the future.

Johnny was a man who clogged himself up; whenever he set a goal, he self sabotaged. He brought up all the pain of the past; he brought out his sack, he emptied it out on the floor and he relived all the disappointments and failures of the past. He had fought in a war that they now say wasn't our country's business. When he came back into civilian life, he had no help adjusting to the real world after living in an unreal world of killing and destruction. He turned his resentment onto his wife, and forced her away from him.

Alone and at the bottom of the pit, he decided to turn his life around. He sought help, was given it, and rebuilt his life. The first part of this process was to let go of the resentment of the people and process that took him to Vietnam. When he could take that first step, he was able to begin his long road home. He was unable to rebuild his marriage, but he is now happily living in a relationship and working in a job of his choice. He lives a happy and balanced life, coping with the ups and downs of everyday living.

Johnny is a man who stopped the 'old movie re-run' and let himself off the hook for the past, for his mistakes. When he did this, he was free to set out in his new direction. To get yourself refocused, acknowledge yourself as being on the right track, forgive yourself for the past, the mistakes and wrong-doings, and move into the future with confidence, hope and enthusiasm.

When it's over, it's over – let it go – move on

~~~

He who forgives ends the quarrel.

AFRICAN PROVERB

Forgive Quickly

☑ Let go of old resentments

☑ Revenge rarely satisfies

☑ Learn from mistakes

☑ Relationships are a wonderful learning ground

☑ When you make mistakes, that's when you need self acceptance the most

☑ Life is about starts and finishes

☑ When it's over, it's over – let it go – move on

Communication

Watch the Borders

THE VEHICLE

You Have To Be Dumb
To Be Smart

Elizabeth's story

Elizabeth's first job came from being at the right place at the right time. She did not have the final exam results or the desire to go on to university, so she was looking for a job. When a friend of a friend recommended her for a clerical position with a firm of accountants and she was offered the job, she took it on the spot without once looking back.

She was enthusiastic and applied herself, and thought she was going very well. She had been in the job for a year and the only part of the job that she did not like was working with Mr Shivers; he was always being a little too familiar with her, like standing way too close to her at the photocopier. He also made sexual remarks, innuendos and asked her personal questions that offended her.

Mr Shivers seemed well respected around the office. He was very good at his job, took a strong interest in the quality of work his staff and got on very well with the other managers.

Elizabeth was naive; she always thought the best of people and wanted to think the best of Mr Shivers, although he was making it very difficult for her to do this. She gently warned him, telling him not to be familiar with her. She tried joking with him in an attempt to kid him out of some of the things he was saying, thinking that a smart reply would shut him up. It didn't, and she realised that it was probably encouraging him even more.

She had no one to talk to about it. She felt betrayed and let down by a person she was meant to respect and be loyal to. The only time she brought it up with the senior office clerk, Beatrice told Elizabeth that she was imagining it, that Mr Shivers was a respectable married man and that such a thing could not possibly happen in this office.

When these things took place, it was long before equal opportunity or discrimination legislation, so there appeared nothing for Elizabeth to do but put up with it.

A year had passed by and the Christmas party was in full swing; everyone was having a great time. The partners were all there with their wives (no female partners in this firm). The fun was simple, silly and totally enjoyable. The night passed quickly. Towards 11.45 pm Mr Shivers came over to Elizabeth and made a pass at her. She reacted as she had done in the past, telling him firmly that he was out of line and to stop putting his hands where they were not wanted.

This time he got angry; the alcohol had kicked in and made him aggressive. Elizabeth's father had always said that alcohol magnifies a person's personality. If they are mean, they become meaner; if they are aggressive, they become more aggressive; if they are a joker, they become more humorous.

Mr Shivers' aggressiveness did not go unnoticed, however. Unbeknown to Mr Shivers, the senior partner, Mr Johnson, happened to be standing nearby and heard the exchange clearly. He moved very quickly; he walked over to Mr Shivers, whispered in his ear, and firmly accompanied him toward the door.

Elizabeth watched them leave and then, through the window, saw their angry exchange of words. Even though she couldn't hear, she could tell that Mr Shivers was protesting very loudly. Soon Mr Johnson marched Mr Shivers over to a cab rank and bundled him very firmly into a cab and sent it on its way.

She arrived at work early the next day, full of trepidation, wondering if it would be her last day. There was no sign of

Elizabeth's story

Mr Shivers and he was usually always in early. She went about her work. At 9.15 am sharp the senior partner asked her into his office.

On his desk was an envelope with her name on it. In those days if there were ever any problems, it was usually the most junior in a company was asked to leave, whoever's fault it was. She took the envelope and, without opening it, started to leave. Mr Johnson stopped her at the door. He asked her to come back and sit down, and when she had, he said to her:

I am very sorry, on behalf of our company, and myself, that this incident has occurred. No one should have to tolerate such behaviour from another person, under any circumstances whatsoever. I am deeply upset that this has occurred within my firm and I hope that you can forgive us for exposing you to such an unacceptable situation.

This envelope contains a formal apology from our firm. Mr Shivers is no longer with this company, so this will not happen to you again. I am led to believe that this is by no means the first time you were subjected to this dreadful behaviour. I only wish that you had reported this to me when it first happened.

Please, Elizabeth, you should never have to put up with that kind of behaviour, ever in your life. You must learn to tell someone in authority if this or anything else unacceptable happens to you again.

Elizabeth left Mr Johnson's office a different young woman to the one who went in. The powerful lesson she had just learnt was to be with her all her life. His kindness, his fairness were of great importance, but the real lesson she

took with her was always to speak up, always speak the truth, even if it meant a risk, a risk in not knowing how the information would be taken.

Mr Johnson may never know the impact his example had on this young woman, how he contributed to her knowledge and wisdom, but in everything she does she communicates her feelings and beliefs clearly and firmly and teaches this truth to others freely.

Years later, looking back at her experience with Mr Shivers, she learnt to feel compassion for him. He had jeopardised his career, his job security, his family life. She understood that some fearsome compulsion must have driven him to be like he was then and she hoped that he too had learnt from the experience, as much as she had.

Elizabeth's story

*Everything I do and say
with anyone
makes a difference.*

GITA BELLIN

You Have To Be Dumb
To Be Smart

Sometimes you have to ask the simple questions to find the right answers. Sometimes you have to ask the seemingly dumb questions to gain the understanding you need. There are many people who are afraid to do this because they are worried that it may make them look ignorant or unknowledgeable, so they choose instead to continue not knowing but appear smart to the outside world. To gain understanding and knowledge, sometimes you have to risk looking dumb; but this tiny risk opens your knowledge and understanding dramatically.

When J. Edgar Hoover, head of the United States FBI in the 1940s, wrote a letter to his agents, his secretary gave it to him for final-edit approval. At the bottom of the letter, he wrote, 'Watch the borders'. The letter was duly sent out to all his agents.

Some weeks later he was surprised and angry to find his manpower budget was sky high. On investigating, he discovered that his agents had taken up the mistaken editing notation he had put there for his secretary and had indeed watched the borders; but for what? This wonderful mistake in communication between Hoover and his secretary had created a step up in security around the nation. Not one of his agents asked, 'Which borders?', 'Why?' or 'For how long?' Not one had the courage to ask Hoover, 'Could you please clarify exactly which borders you want us to watch, for how long, and who are we watching for anyway?'

Ask the questions – take the risk

~~~~~~~

Hoover's agents were afraid to ask the questions for many reasons; they didn't want Hoover to realise that they didn't know what he was talking about, and were afraid to look like they were dumb. This happens so often in everyday life. We fear that our cover will be blown. That people will find out we don't know everything. That we'll look foolish. What if our peers appear to consider us dumb to our faces but are in fact enormously grateful that someone else asked the question because they didn't understand what to do either?

How is it possible to 'open your heart' in the corporate world? This world seems to demand higher productivity from its people, without offering too many solutions about how to go about achieving this aim.

People do want to comply, they do want to contribute, but sometimes old ways of doing things get in the way. Often the message isn't understood or comprehended. Individuals are sometimes unsure of their skills, or their confidence, so their motivation is at a low point, and it can sometimes be easier not to do anything. People get stuck, become victims of non-communication or misunderstandings and unwittingly contribute to the creation of what they fear most – unemployment.

A friend, Sam, had been contributing to a well-known charity for some years as a board member. Sam has a marketing background and was the person who always came up with the creative ways to make money, to get favourable press for the charity, and to gain support in the business community for its fundraisers. Whenever the finance report was being read, he was always very quiet; he listened a great deal and never asked any questions. While this was great for his learning process, often he didn't understand what the figures meant, and like J. Edgar Hoover's people, he was afraid to ask. He was so successful in the areas of marketing and creativity, he was afraid to show his peers that he was relatively naive in the areas of financial management.

Because he hadn't been asking the finance questions all along, it became increasingly difficult for him to do this until, one day, after he had been on the board for years, he decided to take courage. After a long dissertation from the finance person, which left him totally in the dark, he asked his questions. He said later that he could see the relief on the other people's faces all around the table. They hadn't understood, either.

From that meeting on, Sam asked dumb questions, and so did the other board members. He had opened the floodgates to improved communication for all the group by stepping up and risking looking a fool. He and the others reaped the benefits, by better understanding and by increased team respect and productivity.

Don't be afraid to appear dumb or stupid. You may risk appearing not being in control, however, you are less in control if you don't understand the plot.

You can negotiate anything

Herb Cohen, in his book *You Can Negotiate Anything*, says the key to successful communication is in saying simple things like, 'I don't understand' or 'Tell me'. Herb is a consultant to some of the largest corporations and government agencies in North America and teaches at Harvard University. His philosophy is that the more you are prepared to ask, to show your vulnerability and to simplify the process of negotiation (which in essence is only effective communication), the more effective it will be.

In his negotiation seminar, Herb Cohen related an incident in which three Japanese men who were representing a Japanese airline used this process when dealing with a large group of sophisticated executives from an American corporation. The corporation's presentation was large and colourful, and all the latest technology was used to create an impact and present the product in its best light. Starting early in the morning, it lasted two and a half hours, throughout the presentation, the Japanese businessmen sat quietly and said nothing to anyone.

When the presentation was complete, the fresh-faced American presenter, brimming with positive anticipation and expectation, turned to the impassive men from Japan. 'Well...what do you think?'

One of the Japanese smiled politely and answered, 'We don't understand.' The executive's face changed from ruddy to white. 'What do you mean, you don't understand? *What* don't you understand?'

Another of the Japanese businessmen smiled politely and answered, 'The whole thing.'

'From when?' he asked. The third Japanese gentleman smiled politely and answered, 'From when you turned down the lights.'

The executive hunched his shoulders and said listlessly, 'Well...what do you want us to do?'

'Can you go through it again?' replied all three Japanese men.

Wow! How could you repeat a two-and-a-half-hour presentation with anything like the initial vigour and enthusiasm?

Sometimes people get carried away with their own importance and forget there is a listener involved. In this presentation there was too much talking and not enough listening. The Americans didn't read the body language or ask questions; this didn't create an environment for buying ideas or buying the product.

Learn to ask the questions – ask for help

Approaching others by asking for help sets the climate for a mutually beneficial relationship. You'll create an environment which causes the other side to make an investment that is ultimately to both your advantages.

A very successful travel writer, Sol, told me what he believes to be the key to his success as a listener and a communicator. His job is to gain information about the countries and people he visits. 'It is simple,' he said; 'I ask very simple questions, like how, what, where, when, who, why – and a very favourite question of mine is, umm? It allows the person I'm questioning full rein in the conversation and I can really listen and find out more about the person, their culture and their country.'

In my experience, it is not so important to have great talkers to create a successful gathering; it is more important, first, to have great listeners – then great talkers. Often family gatherings are such confusing, unsatisfying events because everyone is transmitting – that is, talking at once – and no one is receiving, or listening. While this serves to create a busy, lively gathering, full of energy, it usually ends up becoming a competition for attention, which is rarely satisfying.

Listening is an essential part of the process of communication, as it was for all of the people I have used as examples in this chapter, but for a large percentage of the population, listening is a challenge. It's a challenge because even before listening becomes a possibility, empathy needs to be exercised.

Walk a mile in my shoes

Empathy is putting yourself into someone else's shoes, walking in someone else's moccasins, seeing the situation from their viewpoint, viewing the problem from their perspective. In creating a situation where you can feel empathy for the other person, first you need to be totally in your body, not thinking about what you will do next or what you need to do later that day. Be totally in that conversation or that listening process, totally with that person, not thinking of other things or visualising other scenarios.

I was giving a talk recently to the caregivers in an aged-care centre about effective communication when in wandered one of the residents, Dorethea. The room was closed for residents, it was for staff only, and she had to exercise a bit of persistence to join us. Dorethea has dementia; her mind cannot function clearly in the present. The past, present and future have become jumbled for her.

145

She can be quite lucid one moment and completely disoriented the next. She can understand where she is, and know and recognise those around her one minute, then feel scared and out of control the next.

She sat down in the front row, and I welcomed her and gave her a workbook. She sat, concentrated and began taking notes, looking at me intensely. She was the first to laugh when I was funny, and she gave me encouragement with her eyes and her smile throughout the presentation.

The notes she wrote weren't decipherable by anyone else; it's unsure just what Dorethea got out of the communication training session, but I am very sure of what I gained from Dorethea. She gave me complete and absolute empathy and total unconditional support. At the end of the day, I realised it was me who had received the workshop. Dorethea reminded me that without empathy, words are just words. What she gave me was from her heart, and that's where you will find your empathy. You will need to use your head to express it, but empathy is felt in the heart and is expressed in the willingness to want to understand and feel what the other person is feeling

Create an equal state of understanding

Effective communication is about bringing two or more viewpoints together in a state of equal understanding. This requires big bucketloads of empathy. It means that for a second, a minute, or longer, you have to view the situation from the other person's perspective.

When communicating, direct eye contact helps you to notice clearly what the other person is saying, what they are thinking and feeling. Notice how they are feeling and imagine how you would be coping, if you were in their situation. Try to build up the empathy by temporarily feeling how they are feeling. Then tell them just how much you are understanding them, with sentences like: 'So when he came into the room and yelled at you at your desk, without any concern for your privacy, this made you very upset' or 'She really made you feel that your opinion was of no value when she ignored you.'

This indicates not only that you understand the subject, but you understand how the person is feeling as well. It gives the person with whom you are communicating the feeling that you care about them.

The reward for patience is patience

Be patient; it takes lots of practice to improve your channels of communication. A person's ability to communicate effectively has very little to do with their intelligence quotient. Just because someone has high intelligence, this does not necessarily make them naturally good at communicating. Schools and universities are full of teachers and lecturers who are poor communicators; they may have enormous knowledge, but they have none of the skills to pass this on.

The teachers who have the greatest impact on students are those who have the ability to inspire the students about a subject by doing two essential things. First, they share their passion about the subject, so that the student is carried along by the enthusiasm of the process. The second key element in being an effective teacher is to be able to adopt creative means by which a message can be repeated over a period of days, not through mindless repetition but by coming at it in different and exciting ways, so that the student will finally get the message.

Between 1879 and 1885 a pioneer in memory research, a German named Professor Herman Ebbinghause, conducted experiments on forgetting. He found that forgetting could be plotted on a graph known as the Ebbinghause Curve of Forgetting. Because of his work in forgetting we now understand a lot more about remembering and about how communication contributes to our remembering.

Repetition is the mother of invention

Professor Ebbinghause's research shows that repetition is essential in order to have good communication. His results indicate that we need to hear a message several times a day for eight days in order for it to be virtually memorised; if these steps are to be followed then at the end of 30 days, the memory retains 90 per cent of that message.

A message read or heard only once is 66 per cent forgotten within 24 hours and is practically out of mind in 30 days.

A message read or heard several times a day for eight days is virtually memorised; at the end of 30 days, the memory retains 90 per cent of the message.

PER CENT
OF MEMORY

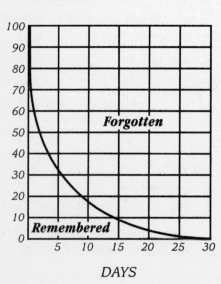

PER CENT
OF MEMORY

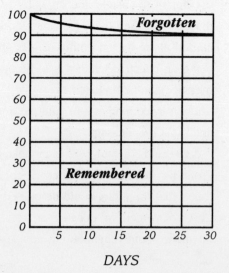

If we do not have an emotional commitment to the message, we need to hear it at least eight times. This explains the frustration of communication a parent has with a child. The parent may have a high commitment to the child having a tidy room, but the child has no commitment to it at all, and hearing the repetitive message 'Please tidy up your room' may not work, because the message is boring, annoying and repetitive. It's important to come at such messages from different perspectives, at different times and in different ways as this can foster that very emotional commitment needed from a child.

Be responsible for how many times you give the message

My friend Bernice doesn't know about Ebbinghause, but overall she considers herself a pretty good communicator. She was very excited recently to have found the perfect hairdresser, Patty. Apart from world peace, one of the most important things in life is finding a great hairdresser. Patty is empathetic, listens to what Bernice wants, is professional, doesn't speak for the sake of filling up the space, and is technically brilliant. Bernice had been along to her six times; six times Bernice explained exactly what she wanted and each time she got it, exactly.

Bernice was feeling very confident when she went to Patty on her seventh visit, so she relaxed; she just sat and enjoyed the experience, giving no instructions at all, just sitting and enjoying. After Patty had coloured and clipped her hair and was giving the final once over, fluffing and scrunching it, Bernice noticed that the colour was a lot darker and that the cut was up at the front and down at the back rather than the other way around. She exclaimed that things were looking a little different than usual and Patty's reply was one of surprise; she had forgotten the six previous visits.

Bernice had to make an appointment to go back and spend another three hours having her hair fixed the way she likes it. She was really angry with herself for not explaining it to Patty again. She knew she should have taken responsibility for doing this, especially when I told her she was only up to number six. This isn't derogatory to Patty; if you walked in Patty's shoes you would understand this. She sees a lot of hair.

Bernice needed to have told her at least two more times, then, perhaps, it would have been permanently etched into Patty's memory bank. It's about bringing your needs to the front of the other person's mind, your priorities to that person's consciousness. When you communicate, it's easy to forget that it's about bringing two sets of thoughts, ideas and feelings together, not separating them; it's about finding common ground.

Begin with the end in mind

Begin with the end in mind; keep your eye on the target, the vision of what you want to achieve. Determine what the end result of the job or task will be and create this in your mind as the target of the communication process. Keep reminding yourself of that end result.

Stay away from playing politics

Stay away from playing politics. The people who play are in the wrong game; they know it and are desperately trying to recruit others into it. Ask yourself whether the advice or instructions they give you will achieve your vision, goal or target. If not, ignore them and their advice. They cannot maintain their game if no one is paying attention to them.

When someone comes to you with some gossip or an intention to stir up negative emotions, it is you who has to guard the gates of your emotions. If someone comes to you with the statement, 'I'm only telling you this for your own good', and you know in your heart that it's not going to be good, it is up to you to say, 'Is it relevant to what we are doing here?' ... 'Is it something that is going to contribute to achieving our aims?' If the answer is no, you will have to find the courage not to get sucked into the game of 'He said/she said/they said'.

Politics, n. *A strife of interests masquerading as a contest of principles.*

AMBROSE BIERCE, *THE DEVILS DICTIONARY*

Take responsibility for the problem and fix it

It doesn't matter who said what at the end of the day. That is an unwinnable game. What matters is whether you have fixed the problem rather than that you have fixed the blame.

Jessie, a 25-year-old university student, was into fixing the blame in a big way. She rarely took responsibility for anything that went wrong, whether it was for running out of petrol – 'The stupid car' – or not doing well in her exams – 'The lecturer set the wrong questions' – or being late – 'My watch is slow, and I'm too poor to have it fixed'. She said she felt it was because she was criticised so much as a child and that no matter what she did, in her Dad's eyes, she could never do anything right, so 'why bother?' We talked about what it could have been like from her Dad's point of view, what could have led him to be like this. She thought about it and then came up with the following scenario:

My Dad's family were very strict; they belonged to a religion that denied any 'earthly pleasures'. We're not talking about Roman orgies here, just dancing and laughing and wearing bright clothes. He was brought up in a very rigid and restricted household.

When he was old enough, Dad left home; he became a rebel with a cause. He travelled the world and tried everything he possibly could, every experience. Every roadway that looked interesting, he went down. He saw poverty in India, he tried drugs in Egypt, he made love to women in almost every country in the world. He saw the good, the bad, the beautiful, the ugly – so much so that when he decided to settle down and marry and have his own children, he felt that he had to protect us from all the pain and hurt of the world. This, added to his conditioning from his early child-hood, was so strong that when he told us not to do things, he did it in a very critical way. His heart was in the right place, but his method was very hurtful, critical and felt very unloving.

Subconsciously, the only way Jessie felt that she could gain her father's love was to create behaviour which would result in him showing his love for her through criticising her for her actions, so it was hard for her to give up not taking responsibility for herself. It meant, on some level, that she would be rejecting her father.

She finally understood that what her father was doing was a form of love, and she decided to talk to him as one adult to another, to see if they could change their pattern. He was communicating love, but so indirectly that it was being interpreted as something else.

So once Jessie had identified the problem, she also took responsibility for fixing it, rather than fixing the blame wholly at her father's feet. If she had just done that, without attempting to fix the problem, her relationship with her father would never have changed.

If your motivation to communicate is low or lacking, take some positive steps, like Jessie decided to do. Look at what is really happening, take responsibility for your feelings as she eventually did, decide on a clear, short-term goal that will give you the ability to change the situation.

Remember your true worth

~~~~~~

Remember your worth – that no matter what happens around you, you are of great value; give yourself that remembrance of your worth. Re-assess your life goals and give yourself a whole day of positive self talk by assessing what you are doing right in the normal, everyday world. By looking at the positive choices you have in every situation, you will find an enormous amount of what is happening is working in your favour. It may take an adjustment of the mind; however, the rewards will give new life to your motivation.

Trust yourself. Trust your ability to solve problems, to be of value. Everything you have seen or heard in your lifetime has been recorded in your brain. It is all there – your wisdom is the combination of your absorption of all of this information plus your intuition. Let it flow.

Trust your intuition

~~~~~~

Intuition is something everyone has at birth; without the help of intuition, our mothers couldn't feed us, and we probably wouldn't have learnt to walk. In communicating with others, listen to the little voice inside for what is not being said too; it's just as valuable.

A.J. Connin wrote of how valuable intuition is in the medical profession. In his series of fictional stories *Dr Finlay's Casebook*, Dr Finlay's mother had come to visit him; he was perplexed about a patient and she gave him some advice that he had not heard before.

His father had been a country general practitioner and had found that the ailment the patient had come to see him about was not always the real problem, but if he really listened, he would hear the real problem and be able to treat it. Often this did not come out until the patient was about to leave the room. He called this the 'door handle diagnosis'.

As the patient laid their hand on the door handle, often they would casually mention the real problem, and more often than not, it had no connection with their original complaint. Dr Finlay's father often treated the problem that they described at the door as they were about to leave, trusting his intuition in the matter, rather than his original diagnosis. He had the courage to change his original opinion and follow his intuition, trusting his wisdom in the moment. Mostly he was proven right.

Part of that flow of intuition and wisdom is also showing your passion. So many people equate passion with sex, but sex is only one of the areas in your life into which you can put passion. Passion can be added, like ingredients in a cake, to love, to friendship, to work, to play, to sport, to music, to art, to literature, to fishing, indeed to anything you do or have in your life.

It is the heart always that sees,
before the head can see.

THOMAS CARLYLE

Find something you have a passion for and do it

Doing something you have a passion for often leads to commitment, as was the case with Winston. His passion was film-making. In his early 20s he had been living very frugally to support his love of film, doing other work to support himself so that he could immerse himself in making films.

A friend of his, Ben, who taught drama at high school level, recognised his passion and asked him to visit his school and to speak to his drama class about film and his love of film. This was an independent school, one that had an open philosophy about education, so the students in the class were interested in all forms of the process of drama, not just acting.

As Winston talked about how film can create images and the influences these have on an audience, Ben noticed his students becoming more and more interested. He noticed the tough kids soften; he noticed the talkative ones listening. He noticed how the room filled with the joy of the subject and spilled out almost into the corridors.

Winston had brought with him his 'love', a Bondex camera, a truly classic tool for a film-maker. He demonstrated it fondly and showed his near reverence for it to the students by lovingly handling it as a precious object. When Ben asked if his students could handle it by actually touching it, a flash of fear hit Winston like a hot ball of fire, bursting in his head. At that point of time he had a choice, either show the students his reverence of it as an object, decline and put it away, or allow them to feel its beauty and its strength and examine it at close range.

The question hung in the room like a scene in a movie in slow motion. Winston was torn, then looked at the students' faces, their emotion kindled by his passion for film, and he made his decision. He later said that at the point of handing it over to the first student, he felt an enormous surge of release. The feeling of *letting go* of something and sharing it was enormously freeing. He has always remembered that, and whenever he talks of his communication process that day, he says that it was the letting go that tested his passion for film and his commitment to being a catalyst for those students.

Two decades have passed. Out of that class, eight students really wanted to do something with their interest in film-making. Winston is still in contact with a handful of those students; they call him for help or advice about their careers or projects. Out of that original eight, six are currently involved directly in the film-making business in Australia and the United States.

Would this have happened if Winston had not demonstrated his passion with the ultimate sharing of his treasured Bondex? Maybe. But it showed how communication is not just the words. It is also the intent behind the words, which Winston demonstrated when he tentatively handed over his camera.

Share your passion willingly

Winston's approach created a wavelength that the students could tune in to and communicate with in a creative way. When you are on that wavelength, time almost stands still. Nothing else matters, just the feeling of pleasure in the enjoyment of the subject.

There is a basic truth about life: 'Whatever you give out, you get back.' This doesn't mean to evaluate everything first, it means letting go: of the Bondex camera, of the outcome, of the possible rewards. People who calculate and measure what is in it for themselves have missed the point; the point is that you create the environment that you would like yourself. Once you have done this, the rewards will come automatically, often from areas or directions you least expected. What you gave out may not have come back from the same person or direction to whom you gave it, but if you are patient, your lifestyle will always reflect your level of commitment to this truth.

Life is a circle:
whatever you put out,
comes back to you

～～～

Seek first to understand, then to be understood.

STEPHEN R. COVEY

Communication

- ☑ Ask the questions – take the risks
- ☑ You can negotiate anything
- ☑ Learn to ask the questions – ask for help
- ☑ Walk a mile in my shoes
- ☑ Create an equal state of understanding
- ☑ The reward for patience is patience
- ☑ Repetition is the mother of invention
- ☑ Be responsible for how many times you give the message
- ☑ Begin with the end in mind
- ☑ Stay away from playing politics
- ☑ Take responsibility for the problem and fix it
- ☑ Remember your true worth
- ☑ Trust your intuition
- ☑ Find something you have a passion for and do it
- ☑ Share your passion willingly
- ☑ Life is a circle: whatever you put out, comes back to you

Love

It's How You Go About It

THE VEHICLE

Building Learning
Relationships

Elizabeth's story

Elizabeth had loved Stuart for five years. In the last year she had felt afraid, afraid that she was making a mistake in staying with him. When they first met, they seemed perfect for each other. They shared similar aspirations and goals; their need to acquire wealth and assets was the same. They had both come from similar working class backgrounds and wanted to turn the tide on their upbringing and conditioning to create enough wealth so that they would not have to struggle like their parents had done.

This was their major link together. They both recognized where they had both come from and both felt that together they could create a future so they would never have to go back there again.

They were young and naïve. He was ambitious, outgoing and fun. They enjoyed building their life together. He provided her with the security that she thought she wanted.

But Elizabeth started to change; she wanted more. She wanted to talk, talk about everything; she wanted to explore thought and philosophy. She wanted to do new and different things.

Stuart, though, wanted things to stay the same. He hated change; he loved order and sameness. Elizabeth was beginning to enjoy exploring new thoughts, new ideas and new experiences. She wanted Stuart to explore these with her.

She tried to tell him that she was not happy. She explained to him over and over that she needed more. He wanted it to go on as before; she wanted it to change. She wanted to expand their horizons, their thinking, the way they interacted, the things they did; he wanted it to stay the same.

She felt that after all the pain of questioning and trying to expand their relationship, there was no chance for the

future – no chance because he was afraid to move on, and she felt she had to move on.

If she were to stay, it would simply mean going over the same discussion and argument, over and over again. It meant, for her, no movement, no growth, no challenge, and for her, these things were the staff of life.

She loved him, but not enough to stay within the boundaries that he wanted. He was shocked when she left – he had not heard her cry – and when he did it was too late. She was gone.

Elizabeth's story

Every person,
all the events of your life
are there because
you have drawn them there.
What you choose to do with them
is up to you.

RICHARD BACH

Building Learning Relationships

Whether it's a relationship with someone we work or play with, whether it's an emotional relationship or a business relationship, getting along with another person is one of life's biggest challenges.

Love is the ultimate acknowledgement

We all crave recognition, to be acknowledged for who or what we are, or what we do. It's a basic need that we sometimes pretend we don't have, but it is alive and well and living deep within all of us. An extension of this need is the ultimate acknowledgement – love – to be loved and appreciated by one special person and to create a partnership with that special one other. The romantic in us searches for our other half, our soul mate.

Women think men want sex. But if we are really honest and listen, we'll find most men want someone to listen to them, to give them compassion, someone to debate with, someone who is sensitive to their needs and will give nurturing and affection.

Men think women want financial and family security. But if we are really honest and listen, we find most women want someone to listen to them, to

163

give them compassion, someone to debate with, someone who is sensitive to their needs and will give nurturing and affection.

So we need to talk with and listen to each other more. It is important, when you do speak, to speak your truth. Your truth is whatever you truly believe at the time – no manifestation or manipulation, no second guessing the other person, just what you truly believe you feel at that moment. And this means not always agreeing with the other person. This may hurt initially; however, if it is your truth at the time then ultimately it will heal the situation, the relationship or the love between you.

Sometimes it may be difficult to access your truth; you may have forgotten it, or hidden it so deep inside that it's hard to remember. This exercise may help you find your truth, but be prepared to listen to the answer.

Accessing your truth exercise

Sit quietly, tucking your bottom firmly into the chair; place your feet flat on the floor and unfold your arms. Close your eyes.

Visualise the scenario that you want to understand. Visualise the person or people involved. Centre yourself, firstly by taking three deep breaths into your abdomen, then by focusing on your heart area. Feel the love, the warmth that emanates from that place and, as you are feeling this, ask your heart to answer the question, your truth, what you need to know.

Sit quietly and drift in and out of that feeling, allowing yourself to be filled with the feeling of love and trust. When you feel you have finished, open your eyes and recall any thoughts or feelings that came to you when you were visualising. If they resonate, like a beautiful piece of music, you may have the answer. It will feel right.

If the answer is not forthcoming right away, that's fine, it will come, be patient. When it does come, it may be in the guise of an article you are reading, or come in a conversation you have in the following days. Or, like it was for me one time, on the back of a bus.

When you hear it, you will know; it will be a giant 'arhhh'. Suddenly you will see what to do. Trust your answer; if it feels right, it will always support you.

Lovers' quarrels strengthen the true bonds of friendship

~~~~~

When you choose a relationship, it gives you both an opportunity to learn very quickly. When you fall in love it can bring out many contrasting emotions. It is natural to be blissful, but love can also produce the opposite feeling. It brings out frustrations, it brings out the differences. Yet it also creates an accelerated learning situation. If you have the courage to learn from the situation, then it really can accelerate your learning.

You need to begin with yourself; you need to tell yourself the truth quickly. Ask yourself what is the real reason you are so angry, or hurt, or resentful. It may take four or five 'asks' before you are prepared to listen honestly to yourself; however, if you haven't the courage to do this, you can't hope to speak the truth with someone else.

Every confrontation is an opportunity to grow within the relationship

~~~~~

Every confrontation with your partner is an opportunity to grow, to learn, to go to the next level of love. But sometimes pain is the entrance price you pay to get to that level.

When involved in a dispute about any differences, misunderstandings or upsets, admit the mistake and take the responsibility for 50 per cent of it. Even if, on the surface, it appears that it wasn't your fault, you contributed to it on some level. Let go of the responsibility of how your partner interprets your message. If you are centred and clear about the issue, then that is the most influential you can be. Let go of how the other person receives the message.

Try not to get into the emotional process of who's right or who's wrong. Go for what the problem is really about and explain your perception of the situation until the other person gets it. It is a matter of taking responsibility for fixing the problem regardless of how it was caused.

Try these questions to get to the true feelings with your partner:

◆ *If this situation were funny, what would you be laughing at?*

◆ *How would you view this situation if you were 20 years older/younger?*

◆ *What would you think or say differently if this were not a problem but an opportunity?*

◆ *What is the larger issue of which this is only a part?*

◆ *What would be happening if this situation meant exactly the opposite of what you think it does?*

◆ *How would you see this situation from the other person's viewpoint?*

◆ *What does the person creating this really want?*

◆ *What emotions are you feeling that are causing you to react, rather than to look at this situation with freshness and creativity?*

These questions will give you other ways of looking at the situation. Perhaps in one or more of the answers you will find a solution or a way of seeing the problem that will give you an opportunity to learn from the differences of opinion and ultimately bring you closer together.

Giving and receiving are the same thing

It is easy to complain about not being given things: flowers, romantic cards or poems; courtesy or respect. A basic principle applies here. Whatever you give out, you get back. So, if you want flowers, be prepared to give them. The days of stereotyped male/female roles are over. You need to give as well as to receive. If you want courtesy, be prepared to give it. If you want respect, be prepared to do what is necessary to give it.

People who want only to receive often become victims and are self-righteous because what they get is never enough, or never the right colour, or the right size. People who want only to give suffer too, because they feel others aren't grateful enough about what they have been given.

You need to be an effective giver, as well as an effective receiver. If you only take one side of the equation, it is easy to become a martyr, and that serves neither person in the relationship. It can be really hard for some people to receive graciously, to be given something and accept it with grace, rather than caution or cynicism, which sometimes sounds like 'Oh yeah, I wonder what he/she wants'. Suspend judgement, accept the generosity. Have the self esteem to accept the complement, kind deed, or gift.

Your ability to do this is a measure of your commitment to the relationship. It is not possible to project yourself into the other person's head to understand what they are thinking anyway, so don't try. Accept the gift, whether a word or deed, as if it were given with the very best of intentions.

I saw an old woman, Adel, sitting at a table at a big family wedding party recently. She sat, as the matriarch of a large family does, with pride and dignity, surrounded by her family of eight grown-up children. I could see by her posture – by the tenseness in her face, the dullness in her eyes – that she had lived a hard life.

As a young girl, Adel was betrothed by arrangement to a man from the same European village. She travelled to Australia, a far off country, a place she did not choose to live, with a man she did not choose to live with, and had to make the best of it. Her life was hard, living through someone else's expectations, never getting it quite right. To deal with this, she suppressed any joy she felt. She closed the door on most feelings altogether. She decided not to receive any happiness or love; she became bitter about the circumstances that life had handed her. She closed down. She closed her heart.

Suppression of joy creates martyrdom

Adel could have chosen a different reaction, a different road. Maybe her reaction was passed on by her mother and she did not feel she had a choice. You don't have to look very far to find joy in this world. But joy needs to be honoured, acknowledged, recognised, before you can feel it. Martyrdom is the continual denial of any of the joyous things happening around you. Look up right now and see all the beauty that surrounds you. It needs to be noticed to have any positive effect on you.

Visualisation exercise

Look around you and settle your eyes on something in nature; look out of the window and look at a cloud. Watch it move, gliding across the front of your vision. See the sky behind it, surrounding it, keeping it safe. Watch the gentleness of the white cloud and how it radiates absolute beauty.

When you watch it for a while, you will notice the light beaming from it. I know it is white to start with, but it is more than that; its vibration is also white and soon sheds a vibrant white light all around it, making it the most beautiful cloud you have seen.

Notice how you are feeling when you are focusing on the cloud; notice that you are feeling warmer, more relaxed and more centred. It is fine to just sit and stare, not to do anything except experience this feeling.

Nature will happily replenish you at any time. It is just a matter of focusing your attention on it, and it is at your disposal. You can never be 'out of exchange' with nature, it will always replenish.

Remember that you can do this exercise with anything. I choose nature because of its infinite beauty, but you can focus your attention on anything; everything vibrates. The chair you're currently sitting on vibrates too if you take the time to focus your attention on it.

Dr John Harrison, in his seminar on Loving Your Disease, gives examples of how suppressing joy over a long period of time creates martyrdom in the person feeling it. Adel did not express her true feelings, which made her numb to anything except a dull pain. So express how you feel, have the courage to say it loud and clear.

Suppressing emotions within a relationship for any length of time, leaving these unresolved or unexpressed, can cause disharmony or disease. If suppressed, emotions like anger can create violence. Left unexpressed, sadness creates misery, and fear that is not dealt with causes chronic anxiety. These emotions, if suppressed, can easily sabotage a relationship. Often the person who feels them in a relationship ignores them and they go away temporarily, but then they bob up again under stress or in unusual situations. The only way of dealing with these effectively is openly and honestly.

The rise in domestic violence is a reflection of our community's inability to deal with the anger that it feels. The culture we have created has taught us to suppress any anger we feel. If a child wants to yell at his or her parent, they have been taught very early that it is naughty and wrong to do it.

Of course, if we went around yelling all the time there may well be chaos, but what if there wasn't? What if the person actually feeling the anger gets the opportunity to express it, deal with the hurt that comes out of it and emerge on the other side of it with some resolve for the future?

Suppression of anger creates violence

Jilly was being medically treated for manic behaviour when I met her. She was in a relationship with a man whom she loved very much, but sometimes out of the blue she would hit out at Ben, the person she loved so dearly. She got so angry sometimes that she physically hurt him: punished him and made him suffer for all the built-up pain and anger she felt.

Ben was confused, hurt and frustrated. He was a reasonably passive man, and never fought back, never lifted a finger, never hurt Jilly in any way.

Jilly discovered in counselling that the anger had little to do with Ben but had a lot to do with the long-term unresolved anger she had felt for over 30 years towards her father. Her father had died five years before, but Jilly's anger toward him had not died.

He had been the best father he could, but he had never let Jilly speak out, never let her say what she felt, never let her express her real self as she was growing up. It had a powerful impact on her and the sessions with the counsellor gave her the opportunity to express it, let it out and move on. It wasn't easy, it took courage on her behalf, but she dealt with it and let it go.

When the anger gets to the violent stage, then the damage has probably already been done, first the damage to the person feeling it, then to the person at whom it's directed. Mostly the person who receives the anger is not the person who caused it in the first place. It has been left to smoulder, to fester and to grow in the mind of the person who felt it and then to suddenly spill out.

Have the courage to deal with the anger when it comes up. Cry, howl, punch a pillow, say it to the person whom you are really feeling it towards or, if that's not possible, say it out loud. Sometimes that works just as well. Just get it out. Medical research is linking more and more sicknesses with suppressed anger, resentment, frustration, guilt and sadness.

Suppression of sadness creates misery

Suppressing sadness can have an equally negative effect on relationships as suppressing anger – sadness leading to misery, leading to depression.

Arthur was a young man who had felt sad most of his life. By the time he was 18 his sadness had escalated into bouts of depression. Every few weeks Arthur became gut-wrenchingly depressed. He explained it as a feeling that absorbed him totally in a negative, fearful way, a way that felt like there was no escape from it. This feeling got in the way of his relationship with his girl-friend Bessy. She was having trouble understanding his depression and wasn't dealing with it very well.

For him, it was a feeling of total isolation and desolation. Aloneness that was inconsolable. At its worse, it felt like a black, hard rock jammed between his chest and his diaphragm, stuck there like a lump of anger, as old as the dinosaur. Whenever he tried to explain it to his parents, they told him, 'Get a grip of yourself, shake yourself out of it.'

'No nonsense' people say that depression is something we all go through, like chicken pox, we just have to get ourselves out of it. They say that unhap-piness, sadness, heartbreak, disappointment and anger are things that all people experience and can be soothed by talking to someone, a good work-out, a 'slam-the-door-in-your-sister's-face', full-on screaming match, rolling around on the floor with your dog licking your face, or getting drunk with your best friend. These things can help, they can assist, they can be a stepping stone. But sometimes true depression is impervious to these practical cures, and the more you try these cures, the more desolate you become.

But the thing that no one ever told Arthur about, the thing that is kept a big secret, is that when you feel so depressed, you want to die – really die. Some people kill themselves when they are depressed.

When you feel that depressed, you have such a low opinion of yourself that you seriously think if you were gone the world would be a better place, because you aren't in it. It is not self indulgent, it is not something you use to get attention or to seem more important than other people; at that point of depression, you think very little of yourself.

Arthur was told to go out and save the world, that he would feel better if he could see the 'worse-off' people, the street kids, the poor. But when he felt depressed, there was absolutely nothing for him to draw on to help himself, let alone anyone else. There was just an emptiness, a void. And he despised himself for it.

His psychiatrist said that it was a cyclical illness that comes and goes, and not necessarily at regular intervals. And the trouble that Arthur had after the feeling lifted was being hopelessly ashamed and guilty for putting everybody through it. Even though people around him loved him and supported him, he still beat himself up mentally for what he thought he must have put them through. So he couldn't win, he wouldn't let himself win, and the times that he felt normal seemed rarer and rarer.

Arthur still gets depressed, but he says it's getting better; sometimes he can go for months and months without it. The ways that he deals with it are varied, often simple, but he's making progress. When he last spoke to me, he was 25 years of age, very bright, interesting, intelligent (in fact, highly intelligent; being smart and getting depressed sometimes go hand-in-hand).

These are the things that help him the most when he gets depressed. Sometimes one thing hits the spot; sometimes he tries them all, sometimes many times over.

◆ *Admit you have a problem. First to yourself, then to someone you trust. If you feel that professional help, such as your GP or a counsellor, would help, see them. Trust your instincts about that. You will never be wrong.*

◆ *Take responsibility for and own your feelings. If that means getting angry, get angry. The same person who got you into it (yourself) is going to get you out of it, so accept responsibility.*

◆ *Be sad, honour your sadness whether it's for a day or an hour. Honour this feeling. Don't try to cover it up, as it only gets worse that way.*

◆ *Try all the surface things – exercise, crying, a good movie, writing your feelings down, whatever is active. Don't pin all your hopes on the immediate outcome. Remember, it took you time to get into this state and it may take time to get out of it.*

◆ *Find a 'listening post', someone with the maturity to listen without judgement. That may be someone outside your family. Sometimes your family members want to 'save you' or 'fix you up' too much to be a good listening post.*

◆ *Reassess your direction or focus in life. Maybe you need more of this or less of that. So discipline yourself to look at what makes you happier and commit to doing more of it when you get out of your depression.*

◆ *Remember that who you are when you are in this state is not your essential nature. It is hard to grasp this, but your essential nature is warm, giving, kind and compassionate; however, it is just not apparent during these times.*

◆ *When you wake up in the morning and there is a glimmer of hope, hang onto it with both hands and build on it straight away with positive self talk.*

◆ *Trust yourself to make the right decision in caring for yourself. Take the opinions of others into consideration, but don't give your power to those people. Trust that the decision you make about the way you will change how you feel is the right one and go with it.*

◆ *Get back in touch with nature. Just sit in it, breathe it in, let it wrap its arms around you and nurture you back into life. Hug a tree, and let it hug you back.*

Suppression of fear creates anxiety

～～～

What you fear most, comes upon you

WILLIAM SHAKESPEARE

Have you ever had your hands full of carefully balanced precious glasses and you hope against hope that you don't drop them, and then you do? Have you been on a roll with a relationship that is going very well and all of a sudden you stop yourself and say, 'This can't last'? Have you ever had a vision of something going wrong and held it in your head just a little too long and it actually happens?

Create positive visual pictures

~~~~~~

It is important to create a visual picture of what it is that you do want as quickly as possible, so that you cancel out the opposite image. It is possible to create the opposite of what you want by imagining it clearly. Remember to check that you are imagining what you desire, not what you fear.

There are two types of fear: the fear that keeps you alive, and the fear that stops you from living. The fears that stop you from living are those fears that step over the line and become phobias. A fear of toads made one North Queensland man move 3400 kilometres south to Victoria. He was too frightened to go out at night for fear of a toad jumping out at him. The toad would undoubtedly have been more frightened of him, but that didn't make the fear he felt any less for him. Burt, a man in his late 30s, has a fear of being rejected, so he never commits in a relationship or loves another person, because he was hurt deeply as a teenager by his first love.

Rebecca Gibney, famous for her role as Emma in *The Flying Doctors* series, in an interview with Mike Safe in the *Weekend Magazine*, told of her anxiety attacks. Since her teens, she has suffered anxiety attacks; she says she manages to keep them under control, but when she feels stressed, these anxiety attacks can stop her from working.

She talked about how when under a lot of stress, she feels a loss of control which frightens her, and that her fragile self image influences her ability to handle it, or not handle it. She said that, for her, putting on her make-up was like wearing a mask. But no matter how much she changes role for a part, when she wakes up in the mornings and looks at herself in the mirror, she still sees herself as a 15-year-old fat kid with cellulite, pimples and stringy hair, which is nothing like the reality.

Rebecca is a very special person; she is able to give pleasure to so many people through her acting. But she is one of many hundreds of thousands of young people who have this fear that has turned into an anxiety which manifests itself as sporadic anxiety attacks. So in some small or large way, these fears stop these people from living lives where and how they want.

Then there are fears that keep you alive; they are the danger warnings. They make you wear a lifejacket on a boat in open water, not go too near the edge of a steep cliff, and look to the right and left before walking out on to the road. These fears are there to keep you alive, not to stop you from living.

Focus on your goals
not your fears

Examine your fears carefully. Which are serving you? Which are you serving? The ones that you are serving, that give you nothing but anxiety, are those that you need to examine and let go of. If they are not serving you, you may be in a chronic state of anxiety about them and the world. It is very difficult to have an equal relationship with anyone if one of you is giving your power away to fear, or suffering chronic anxiety.

Those who suffer the most with chronic anxiety are those who constantly notice all the wrong-doing in the world. They complain about it bitterly, but choose to do nothing about it. They are great identifiers of wrong-doing, and they say things like 'Isn't the world a terrible place because of ...' The 'because of...' changes daily, as there is always some other fear to be identified.

I gain strength, courage and confidence
by every experience in which I must stop
and look fear in the face.

ELEANOR ROOSEVELT

Be proactive not reactive

~~~~~

Those who identify the problems and are prepared to do something about them are fear proactive, not reactive. They are doing something with their fears that is positive. Don't get trapped into old fears, those that are not serving your wellbeing. Let go of them, face them or deal with them. You have nothing to lose if they are not life-threatening fears, and everything to gain.

Relationships create a wonderful playing field

~~~~~

Emotions such as anger, sadness and fear come up in relationships because a one-to-one relationship is so intimate that anything that is not going to serve it may come up to sabotage it. Deal with the issues. Relationships create a wonderful playing field for healing many old wounds. You have a choice about how you deal with the future. Use these old emotions to make new and better choices for your future relationships.

Build an action plan for effective relationships

~~~~~

To build relationships with your partner, your spouse, your lover, your best friend, focus on the following areas to heighten the closeness, the bond that exists between you.

◆ *Actively listen, be in your body. Turn around and face the person you are speaking to. The washing up is not as important as the relationship. Face that person and give them your undivided attention. Show them not just in your words, but also in your body language that you care about what they are saying.*

◆ *Use the 80/20 rule. Approximately 80 per cent of the relationship is great. Twenty per cent may be difficult, unhappy, or involve making mistakes or learning. Try spending 80 per cent of your self talk on the things that are going right with that person and 20 per cent fixing the mistakes. If you spend all the time picking at the 20 per cent, it will soon become more than 20 per cent, and when this happens, the disintegration of the relationship is not far behind.*

◆ *Perception is reality. If you perceive the other person as always wrong, then that becomes your reality. Change it, look at the positive; focus on the 80 per cent that works in the person and in the relationship. Catch your partner doing things right 80 per cent of the time, then that becomes reality.*

◆ *Before attacking the other person about an issue, be prepared to look in the mirror first and ask two questions: 'Do I do this myself?' and 'What am I afraid of?' If you are attacking the person for something that in fact you also do yourself, and you are not prepared to deal with this issue within yourself, then you are not being 100 per cent honest and will not be able to resolve this issue with your partner. Sometimes we attack the other party about a small issue because we are afraid of a bigger issue and need to take the focus away from what really matters. Be prepared to look at the big picture and deal with what's really bugging you, then stand back and reap the rewards.*

Talk past the point of pain

~~~~~~~

◆ *Face the fear. Talk past the point of pain. Keep asking why. Often people are conditioned not to create conflict because they were taught that it is 'not nice'. Conflict is part of life. Look at history. Before any change or growth takes place, there is usually conflict.*

◆ *Make your point of view clear and understood, not just negatively. It can only become positive when you have taken the plunge to talk past the point of pain, past the point of politeness, past the point of saying the right thing. Social consciousness has a lot to answer for. Break through the* shoulds *and* shouldn'ts *and tell the person your true feelings. Talk past that point of pain.*

◆ *Remember to respect the feelings of the other person. Don't expect them necessarily to agree with you. Respect the way they feel. Their perception is* their reality.

◆ *Keep nurturing you own self esteem. It's difficult to help someone else if you are not prepared to build your own base of self value first. Remember to give yourself clear, positive self talk. Often when two people are in conflict, it is easy to attack the other's self worth. Guard your self worth as if it were a precious gem; without it you are of no value to yourself or the other person.*

◆ *Give up being right. Do you want to achieve the goal, which is a caring loving relationship, or do you want to be right, saying, 'I told you so' or 'I knew that would happen'? This* doesn't serve the relationship at all. Go for the goal of a loving relationship and give up being right.

◆ Speak the truth as quickly as possible. Sometimes that's hard, because you don't even know what the truth of the matter is yourself. Go with what feels right. Trust your feelings, your wisdom and your knowledge and let that flow.

◆ Centre yourself, take deep breaths into your diaphragm. When you centre yourself physically, you can be in control in the midst of confusion. Many of the martial arts use centring as a way of accessing unused power. It is available to you at any and all times. Focus on your diaphragm and take deep breaths to push your diaphragm out as far as it will go, then fill your lungs to capacity and slowly exhale. Do this several times to bring you back into your own power.

◆ Turn off the TV, turn on the music – it cuts straight to the heart. Music has a way of filling the spirit with love. It doesn't matter what kind of music it is, just as long as you and your partner love it. It creates an atmosphere for love and understanding like nothing else.

◆ Walk, ride, play golf, read – do something together. It's not even important to talk while you're doing it. It's the sharing of the experience that is important.

Love is everything. It is the key to life, and its influences are those that move the world.

RALPH WALDO TRINE

*People are unreasonable, illogical, and
self-centered. Love them anyway.
If you do good, people may accuse you of
selfish motives. Do good anyway.
If you are successful, you may win false friends
and true enemies. Succeed anyway.
The good you do today may be forgotten
tomorrow. Do good anyway.
Honesty and transparency make you vulnerable.
Be honest and transparent anyway.
What you spend years building may be
destroyed overnight. Build anyway.
People who really want help may attack you
if you help them. Help them anyway.
Give the world the best you have and you may
get hurt. Give the world your best anyway.
The world is full of conflict.
Choose peace of mind anyway.*

ANONYMOUS

Have the courage to ask the questions, to shift the barriers, to move on

How will you know if your relationship with your partner is finished? This is a question you will ask yourself at least once in your lifetime. If you have learnt everything you can from this person, both negative and positive, and all you are doing is going over the same hurt, the same experiences, without any growth or movement, then you have probably been as valuable to each other as you can.

When I was first married, some friends at our wedding, Vince and Loretta, were telling us how they had been married for 21 years and that we should 'just wait till you have been married as long as we have', as if it were some sort of trophy – some sort of grand achievement. It was. Except they had created a relationship of co-dependency, a relationship where she depended on him, and he on her, not in a growing, equal way, but in a way that was totally enslaving. They could not function well as individuals apart, only collectively, together. They had a life of *having* to depend on each other, not especially wanting to, but accepting it as part of the price to pay in a marriage.

Mr and Mrs Jones had a similar story. They had their 60th wedding anniversary party in the local church hall recently, put on by their family with great enthusiasm. They had all the family together, three generations in all. Mr and Mrs Jones did not touch each other, say a kind word, glance an encouraging glance to each other; they lived in two entirely different worlds, never interconnecting, never sharing.

The surprising element of it all was that they were separately proud of the fact they had been married for 60 years. Strange. They had no relationship, no shared pleasure or joy, they had barely spoken to each other for 20 years, but they were proud of the number sixty. Sixty years of what? Sixty years of the same experience year after year. No growth, no shared pleasure, no emotional unity. What were they celebrating? A number, not a lifetime of happiness.

They were totally immersed in a game of mutual suffering and punishment, the role of co-dependency. They did not have the courage to let go of their negative relationship and move on to something else, something to share, to grow with, to have as an example of pleasure for their children.

All relationships, wonderfully, have the potential for success and pleasure. However, where do we get the idea that relationships have to be perfect all the time? An honest relationship is a growing thing – it's not possible for something that is growing to be perfect all the time.

Love is a moving target

You might get some aspect of your relationship right and another part changes, or your opinion or perspective changes. Love is a moving target, it does not need to be made perfect – love already is. It is the acknowledgement of love that makes it blossom and grow – the acknowledgement of yourself and your partner as valuable and worthwhile people, both growing together, but separately, toward learning and knowledge, through the experience that love creates.

Acknowledge your children

Acknowledging children for their true value is very important too, particularity if you are a parent. It is not always easy doing this, but children can be our best teachers, if we have the ability to listen to their wisdom, to their contribution. Because they are so much closer to the source, birth, they have a naïve wisdom that, if respected, will grow and enrich everyone around them, not just the immediate family.

Let your children make mistakes. Let them learn. Don't let them try anything that is dangerous or life threatening, but let them learn the natural way through mistakes. Parents who are over-protective of their children make them dependent and that serves neither the child nor the parent.

Talk to children with respect; they understand. If you talk to them like babies (even when they are babies), they will want to stay that way because they are rewarded for it. How often have you seen a child in his or her late teens still hanging on to their baby voice because it is such a valuable tool for gaining attention. A child needs to grow and to grow up. Speak to them as you would like to be spoken to.

A loving parent knows that they and the child have separate lives and are happy to focus on their own lives while supporting their child in theirs. Children don't become perfect, they just get better with experience. If you let them, that is.

Argue for your limitations,
and sure enough, they're yours.

RICHARD BACH

Take responsibility for your life, so your children can for theirs

Let children take responsibility for their lives, their decisions, their consequences. This means that parents need to take responsibility for their own lives first. Children learn best by their parents' example. It is hard not to model. Whether we like it or not, we are great modellers on our parents. Some of the traits you may hate the most, you may end up repeating.

Imitation

If a child lives with criticism,
he learns to condemn
If a child lives with hostility, he learns to fight
If a child lives with abuse, he learns to hurt others
If a child lives with encouragement,
he learns to be confident
If a child lives with fairness, he learns to be just
If a child lives with tolerance,
he learns to be patient
If a child lives with approval,
he learns to like himself
If a child lives with love,
he learns to find love in the world

ANONYMOUS

You cannot *not* model behaviour

~~~~~

Josh, a young man in his 11th year at school, was allocated to a solicitors' office for his week of work experience as part of his education process. He was delighted; his Dad was a solicitor and he was happy to be following in his Dad's footsteps.

It was with great surprise that two hours into day one, the school received an anxious call from the solicitors' office to come and collect the young man. When the teacher arrived to collect Josh, he found him sitting outside one of the senior partner's office with his arms firmly folded and an expression of absolute distaste on his face.

The teacher was embarrassed, but only became more so when he found out why Josh was on strike. Josh had been allocated a woman solicitor as his mentor for the week's work experience. Nothing unusual about that, except that Josh's father had told him all his life that women were only 'good as two things in this world, secretaries and mothers'.

No amount of counselling over the next year could budge Josh's feelings about this issue. The example from his father was too strong. After he graduated as a solicitor, Josh found a job in his father's law firm, where the only women there work as secretaries. Was it honest for Josh's father to teach him sexism? Josh decided not to unlearn it and is still working with his Dad.

Honesty is an issue that scares parents the world over. 'How honest should I be with my child?'. There are no degrees of honesty. Honesty just is. It sets the scene for children to be honest in turn with their children, and so on.

To love children is to have the courage to let go, to show by example what you expect, and to listen with love, not judgement. It doesn't seem like a lot, but in its practical application it needs a consistency that many adults don't even have for themselves, let alone for their offspring.

Support your children while they make mistakes

~~~

With kids, it is what you do most of the time that counts. Getting it right 100 per cent of the time is a myth. There is a joke that goes like this: 'Why do they give the two most important jobs in the world to totally inexperienced people, politicians and parents?' That's it - not very funny, but it has a ring of truth to it. Just do your best; don't go for perfection. Support your children while they are making mistakes. It is what you do most of the time that counts. So if you are a pretty terrific parent most of the time, then you've succeeded.

Congratulations!

Share your love with generosity

~~~

The bond that links your true family
is not one of blood, but
of respect and joy in each other's life.
Rarely do members of one family
grow up under the same roof.

RICHARD BACH

Building Learning Relationships

- ☑ Love is the ultimate acknowledgement
- ☑ Lovers' quarrels strengthen the true bonds of friendship
- ☑ Every confrontation is an opportunity to grow within the relationship
- ☑ Giving and receiving are the same thing
- ☑ Suppression of joy creates martyrdom
- ☑ Suppression of anger creates violence
- ☑ Suppression of sadness creates misery
- ☑ Suppression of fear creates anxiety
- ☑ Create positive visual pictures
- ☑ Focus on your goals not your fears
- ☑ Be proactive not reactive
- ☑ Relationships create a wonderful playing field
- ☑ Build an action plan for effective relationships
- ☑ Talk past the point of pain
- ☑ Have the courage to ask the questions, to shift the barriers, to move on
- ☑ Love is a moving target
- ☑ Acknowledge your children
- ☑ Take responsibility for your life, so your children can for theirs
- ☑ You cannot *not* model behaviour
- ☑ Support your children while they make mistakes
- ☑ Share your love with generosity

Be Outrageous

---

*Life's Not What
You Think It's About*

THE VEHICLE

Creative Thinking

Elizabeth's story

Elizabeth was on her own. It was her choice, but for the first time in her adult life she had no brothers and sisters or father to care for, no husband, just her, and it was hard. She hadn't supported herself for several years – she hadn't had to, Stuart had looked after her – and here she was alone and frightened. It may have been her choice, but she was still frightened.

She stayed that way for a while. She became a 'poor me' for a couple of months. Then she hit rock bottom; one morning she found herself drinking a double Scotch for breakfast with her cornflakes. That was the final straw. She decided to take action.

She reached for the newspaper, opened the job search section and began the process of finding a job. But nothing she was interviewed for was right, either from her perspective, or that of the employer. She found herself unemployable, or at least it looked that way.

The thought of taking any welfare benefits was anathema to her. She was far too independent for that. The only way out for her was to start her own business. She didn't have a cent to her name, or any idea of where to begin, but she had nothing to lose and everything to gain.

Elizabeth started by thinking about what she enjoyed doing. Being a very visual person, she took a large piece of paper and lots of crayons and drew all her thoughts regarding what she liked to do. Then she played with the ideas on the sheet of paper, took out some more paper and further expanded some of the ideas. She did this all day. She didn't notice the time passing, she was having so much fun creating all her ideas.

It was nightfall when she stopped, mainly because her train of thought was interrupted by having to put on the light. She viewed her work. She knew there was an idea

there that would become her future, but she was still afraid to make a decision. Elizabeth decided to sleep on it.

Strangely, she slept well; she woke up refreshed, motivated, happy. For the first time in years she felt clear and fresh. She took this as a positive omen. There must be an answer for my future in my ideas, she thought.

This time when she looked at her ideas, she became more analytical and logical about them, putting all the ideas she liked on one side of the paper and eliminating the others as she went. On the other side of the paper she started writing what action she could begin, in order to take the ideas to the next step.

Pretty soon she had three great ideas for a business, and three corresponding action plans that she could start working on to turn these ideas into income. Eventually, she couldn't decide between a mobile secretarial service and a home catering service.

She sat back and, one at a time, visualised herself running these businesses. She liked the idea of both. She then visualised how the business would be in five years. She let her creative mind take over and project the future. She had her answer. The visualisation of her catering business showed her having more fun, enjoying herself more, and making other people happy in the process.

The decision was made. Her creative mind had helped her make her final decision. She was excited, scared, but ready. That day she created Lizzie's Home Made Food Company. She has never looked back.

Elizabeth's story

*I used to think that anyone
doing anything 'weird' was 'weird'.
I suddenly realised that anyone
doing anything 'weird' wasn't 'weird' at all,
and it was the people saying
they were 'weird' that were 'weird'.*

PAUL McCARTNEY

Creative Thinking

～～～

Wouldn't it be wonderful if you could take the vigour and enthusiasm of child-hood with you into your adult life? Wouldn't it be great if you could see every colour, shape and size with the same clear, non-judgemental eyes? Wouldn't it be fantastic if you could take more chances, like a child taking its first step, and look at the world with wide 'baby eyes'? To be able to take that naïvety into our sophisticated world and use that freshness, that vitality in the stuffy corridors of life, breathing fresh air into the hearts and minds of others.

Humour is creative thinking at work

～～～

Creative thinking is relating things and ideas which were previously unrelated. The use of humour is a fine example of this. A group of intern nurses were asked on their first day, 'Why do the doctors need to wear masks while they are operating?'; back came the reply 'Well, if they make a mess of it, no one will know who did it.' Everyone laughs because the answer was unexpected. Creative thinking is often an unexpected idea surfacing that is exactly the right answer, the right direction or path to take.

To increase the use of your creative mind, it helps if you understand the relationship between left and right brain thinking. The two halves of the human brain are called left and right hemispheres. In a manner of speaking, we have two minds. Getting to know both sides of your brain is an important step in liberating your creative potential. The left hemisphere controls the right-hand side of the body and is predominantly linear, logical, symbolic and analytical. The right hemisphere controls the left-hand side of the body and is predominantly creative, vision and dream oriented, and intuitive.

I believe that there is a creative genius in all of us waiting to be expressed. If you understand the left and right hemisphere functions, and know how and when to use them effectively, you will unleash your creative potential.

Identifying left and right brain thinking

The left brain has one-at-a-time processing, is sequential (e.g. A, B, C, D, E, F, G), looks at the detail (e.g. on the face, it will look at a freckle), is logical (looks for cause and effect), charts information and produces linear thinking. It relies heavily on previously accumulated, organised information and has the power of grammatically stringing words together. The left brain knows *how* to do things, and is expressive in logical words and sentences. It talks to you all the time, as in a running commentary.

The right hemisphere is creative, visionary, visual, holistic, non-verbal and intuitive. The right brain has all-at-once processing, is simultaneous (sees a complex image), looks at the whole (a face, not just a freckle), connects the world into related wholes, sees correspondences and resemblances, is receptive to qualitative, unbounded aspects of the world and is a feeling state.

The right brain produces imaginative thinking, charts emotional differences of thought, responds to words as images, as in the words of a song, poem or jingle, knows *what*, can remember complex images, doesn't talk to you, uses pictures not words.

As children we use our creativity freely; we make up poems, songs and grand works of art (at least they feel like that at the time). When did you give up the idea of being a poet or a great painter? As a child you made up things, wrote, drew, acted, pretended to be other people. It's so sad that adults decide to be sensible, join the status quo and lose the ability to trust their intuition and their naturally inherent creativity. We all start out as writers, actors, poets, but lose this ability when we grow up, perhaps even give it away.

Intuition and creativity go hand in hand

When you intuitively think of a creative idea, this comes from the right brain. It can occur anywhere – in the shower, driving the car, on waking in the morning, sitting in nature, staring into space, during a meeting, wherever you are – when you stop consciously thinking.

Many creative people talk of the creative space in their head; some people call it the gap between their thoughts, a place where they let go of linear thinking and drift in space. Maybe it is like a coffee house where all the minds on this planet meet and suspend their controlled thought, let go and access each other's creativity. Perhaps it may even be accessing universal thought. In between the structured, controlled thoughts, the gap contains infinite wisdom.

Visualisation exercise

Close your eyes and focus your attention on relaxing each part of your body, starting at your toes and finishing at the tip of your head. Have the clear intention of 'letting go' when you begin this exercise.

Let go of your attachment to the outcome, because chasing the outcome or getting attached to it means that you will come back into conscious thought. Let go of all control and allow your thoughts to drift off. They will be very busy at first, going in lots of different directions; that's fine, just let this happen. Remember to still the mind. Think of nothing. Let go.

195

Allow this process about five minutes at first, then, when you feel the gap, allow yourself to stay in it for longer. It works well if you can sit in nature to do this exercise. The freedom of nature sets up the atmosphere for you to access your creative mind easily.

In this exercise you just allow the creative process to exist, but don't be surprised if you also access some creative thoughts afterwards. Some solution to a problem or difficulty may magically appear after you have discovered the gap between your thoughts.

We have far more potential in life for achieving our dreams if we access the creative mind, the right brain, the gap, or whatever you perceive it to be. And this process can be used for putting information in, taking it out, or letting go.

90 per cent of today's thoughts were also thought yesterday – think again.

DEEPAK CHOPRA

Once you have accessed ideas or information, it is very important to *play* with them first, like a kitten with a ball of string. Allow your wild thought patterns to expand. Play with them. Don't use your logical mind before you have lots of fun with them. We all too readily judge, evaluate and measure these ideas before we have given them a chance to breathe, to grow, and to develop.

Inventions as crazy as the pet rock would never have been invented if such wild ideas had been judged too quickly. When Post-it note pads were invented at the end of 1978, 3M conducted market research which showed that the product would be a big flop. But the inventor used the same wild ideas that created the product to create the interest in the product. He accessed the market place by using his right brain, his creative function.

He sent free samples out to the personal assistants of all of the chief executive officers of the Fortune 500 companies, the leading 500 US companies in innovation, research, development and growth in their respective fields at that time. The CEOs all of a sudden found they were getting reports and letters that had these little Post-it notes stuck fast, but temporarily, on their correspondence. Their personal assistants had started to use them and had started to become addicted to the sticky yellow notes. The CEOs requested that their personal assistants order more, and they weren't even on the market yet.

The 3M company was forced to sell them, following on from the clever marketing ploy of the inventor. Interestingly enough, this product is the product most sold by 3M, and sales are still growing. And this was all because the inventor didn't give up. He continued to play with the idea until he created critical mass. Critical mass is when enough people run with an idea until it 'takes off' all by itself.

In 1938, after six years' work inventing the modern photocopying process, Chester Carlson was unable to sell his invention. Until 1945 he had no response from such companies as IBM and Kodak. Only a non-profit institution, Battelle, was willing to invest in this wild idea. Carlson convinced them of its value in the marketplace and, with them both playing together with the wild idea, they marketed a process which is used in almost every office in the world today.

Be still. Close your eyes. Listen. Ask the questions you need the answers for, then listen to what your creative mind throws up. All of the above successes were crazy, lunatic, mad ideas. Your mind will not throw up an idea which it doesn't have the ability to solve or create. It's just that most of us give up on the creative process too soon, rather than trusting it. Listen, play, listen again, then act on what you have imagined in your creative or right-brain pattern. Where do you think these words are coming from right now?

Recognise opportunity

In developing creative ideas there are three steps: recognising opportunity, creating opportunity and becoming the opportunity.

Once you have recognised the idea, the concept, the wild thought and played with it for a while, you then develop the opportunity by creating the next step, which is following up, research and development, brainstorming, getting other like-minded people involved. Then the idea becomes opportunity as more people become involved to create the critical mass needed to put the idea in place.

The left-brain function is essential because without it the dreams just stay as dreams. Without the left-brain follow up and action, the dream does not become an achievement. That's the difference between dreamers and achievers. The dreamers are always 'gonna', 'should have', 'why didn't I?', whereas the achievers take the next step into *action*.

Move freely from right to left brain, then back to right again

Movement needs to occur from right to left brain and back again freely for creative thinking to be effective. Both hemispheres work as a team: the right creating, then the left actioning that creative idea. So use both sides of the brain, moving your thoughts from right to left then back to right again. This will utilise your whole brain.

The right side comes up with the creative, imaginative, exploring, intuitive ideas. Then these are passed over to the left side for action, using logic and rational, deciding skills. Ideas pass from the right hemisphere, which is harmonious, optimistic, connected, enthusiastic, and full of wonder, to the left side, which is judging, reactive, egotistic and cynical. When both sides of the brain are employed, the balance of ideas is complete.

Often people favour one side of their brain to the detriment of the total picture. By using the left side only, no new ideas can grow or new ground be broken, no new vision implemented. So using right then left then going back to right again is essential in setting the idea into action.

In creating new beliefs, the right hemisphere creates abundance, the potential; it explores new ideas, creates the future through future vision, and is totally non-judgemental. The left hemisphere, on the other hand, is judgemental, anxious and suspicious of the new, and limits the future. So in accessing the right brain we create the future, then by accessing the left we measure it, balance it and put it in place, by actioning it. Turning it back over to the right side is then essential for achieving any new vision, as the right knows no boundaries.

Expect a miracle

The reason that you need to go back to the right brain after you have used the *action* left-brain function is to use the *miracle* part of the process. This part of the process is extremely significant. It is believing without the evidence. All of the great inventors had it. They were criticised, they were laughed at, they were hounded out of their profession and their society. But nothing could stop their belief that they had an idea that would work, an idea whose time had come.

How much belief would you be prepared to put behind an idea that you had created? How much would you be prepared to risk to follow your dream, your truth, against all society? That sort of defiance is believing without the evidence. Without it, the idea or dream will peter out and become nothingness. You must believe in miracles for the creative idea to eventuate. Nothing else has this power, this ability, to make your dream come true.

Miracles can always do with a bit of encouragement. From the following nine points, choose the ideas you need to work with to create a miracle-friendly environment for you.

You seek problems because you need their gifts.

RICHARD BACH

1. Challenge the rules

Often, the amount a person uses her imagination is inversely proportional to the amount of punishment she will receive for using it.

ROGER VON OECH

Roger Von Oech reminds us with this quote how, as children, we were encouraged not to break the rules. We were taught that the whole basis of our society revolved around not *rocking the boat*, not *going outside the square*, that if we did break the rules we would be punished. But, more and more, evidence shows us that to use our whole brain, especially in our adult lives, we need to challenge the rules constantly.

If you follow *old* rules just because they are in place, if you are doing things just because you have always done them that way, then you need to examine how you make decisions today and revise any rules that do not serve you any longer. Originally, you probably made the guidelines based on good sense. But as time passes and things change, so do opportunities – unless you are prepared to examine the original reason for making the guidelines and have the vision to change them when they don't serve your real purpose any more.

I knew of a government department that until six months ago was still taking the tea trolley around to each floor, dispensing tea and biscuits at regular intervals, once at 10.00 am for morning tea time, once at 1.30 pm for the after-lunch cuppa, and again at 3.15 pm for afternoon tea time. This was originally an appropriate idea, as it suited the habits and the mindset of the department 70 years ago. However, it had become too rigid a process to suit the people now. With work centring mostly around computer processing in that department, it became imperative to have regular breaks away from the computer screens. It was better for staff members to get up, take a stretch and as a form of break, make a cup of tea or get a glass of water.

Another part of the tradition had also changed. People now have such a vast range of personal preferences about what they drink that only 50 per cent were availing themselves of the tea or coffee on the tea trolley. When a time and motion study was carried out, it was not only found that it was costing an unrealistic amount of money, it was also not serving the consumers. Their tastes and habits had changed and no one had noticed or taken any trouble to change the products to meet the needs of the consumers.

Roger Von Oech highlights the story about the Macedonian general, Alexander, in the year 333 BC, arriving with his army and large following in the Asian city of Gordium. Alexander heard about the local legend surrounding the town's famous knot, the 'Gordian Knot'. The prophecy stated that whoever was able to untie this intensely complicated knot would become King of Asia. History tells us that Alexander loved a challenge. He thought this was an ideal way of becoming the King of Asia, so he attempted to untie it. He tried every traditional method of untying the knot, but to no avail.

Suddenly he had an idea. He pulled out his sword and he cut the knot in half. He made up his own knot-untying rules! Asia was his.

> *Every act of creation is first of all*
> *an act of destruction.*

PABLO PICASSO

As long as you don't hurt someone or break the law, you must challenge assumptions, challenge the rules. Your thinking is only rejuvenated if you have the ability to see what could be. And it is difficult to see what could be if you are locked in to old rules just because they have always been there. Don't follow blind assumptions. If you do follow assumptions, make sure they are your assumptions, based on your thoughts and creativity.

2. *Trust your dreams*

Do you remember your dreams? Do you wake up and ever wonder whether you dreamt something or whether it actually happened? Do you ever wake up with a clear insight about something you have dreamt about? Everyone has these abilities, but if they are not remembered or acted upon, pretty soon you lose the ability to use dreaming as a tool.

Have you ever dreamt that you or someone you know has died? People can interpret this as very negative but it usually symbolises the death of an idea or a relationship. It is extremely rare that a person sees or dreams of their death.

Most dreams are symbolic, they represent something you are consciously or subconsciously working through at the time. Look for what the dream represents. Here are some interpretations that I have found helped me to see the message in my dreams, enabling me to learn from them:

◆ CLOUDS
Clouds can indicate drifting through life, not taking thorough responsibility for where you are in life.

◆ CAR
Always indicates for me my journey through life. Look at who is in the car with you, how you are getting along with them. Look at the condition of the car, inside and out. It may give you a few hints about how you are travelling and what you need to do at the time.

If your car is falling to bits, it may mean that you need to stop and give yourself some attention. If you are having an accident, look at whether you are taking charge of your life, and take steps to take back control of your life.

◆ WATER
Can be about how things are travelling around you. Is the water murky or clear? Are you gliding through the water, or

are you in choppy waves? This dream can be used to centre yourself, to enable you to take control of the circumstances around you.

◆ ANIMALS
Represent the kingdom of nature, and how you are respecting it. If the animals are kind and accepting, you are in a flowing relationship with the natural elements. If they are scary or aggressive, then you may be pulling against the flow of nature and may need to realign your thought pattern or your behaviour toward nature.

There are plenty of reference books about dream interpretation. One we use in our family a lot is Denise Linn's *Pocketful of Dreams*. Use this reference or others; there are many of them. Choose your own interpretation; that's usually the most accurate. Look for the positive. Dream interpretation is much like life. If you interpret life in the positive, that's what it mostly gives you. If you interpret life in the negative, that's what it mostly gives you.

See your dreams in the big picture of your life. The more you remember your dreams, the more you will dream. If you wish to remember your dreams as you go to sleep at night, ask yourself to wake remembering your dreams. You will be amazed at how well this works.

Lao Tzu fell asleep and dreamt he was a butterfly. Upon waking he asked, 'Am I a man who has just been dreaming that he was a butterfly or a sleeping butterfly dreaming he is a man?

LAO TZU

203

3. Develop 'all round' vision

'All round' vision is the ability to see where you have been, where you are going and where you are, all at the same time. Flies have it, the ability to see everything at once.

Notice what is going around you. See the coincidences that are occurring. See the opportunities that show themselves. See the patterns of your life. If you are not happy with the patterns, change your reaction, but honour the opportunities around you by acting upon them. Often it is enough just to notice them.

I work in the training business. I work with private and public organisations, advising and training their teams about customer service and team building. People are always giving me suggestions about who could benefit from my training, saying things like: 'Boy, do XYZ Company need you. Their customer service is awful. You should approach them.' Very rarely is it appropriate to do this. I doubt that any company would respond favourably to someone coming into their business telling them what is wrong with them. And rightly so. However, I always listen to the suggestions, just in case something comes up in my own 'all round' vision.

I had such a suggestion from Charles, an associate in business. He said to me one day, 'I'm working with ABC Company. It is so hard to implement the changes we are going for; the staff are so demotivated. It would be wonderful if you could teach them the skills of self motivation, that would be really helpful.' He recommended me to them, but the person who would make that decision was so demotivated he couldn't see the point.

A week later I saw an article in the paper about this company. Two days later I was sitting in a traffic jam with an advertisement for that company's product staring at me for five minutes. My daughter came home and told me about a work experience talk they had at school about this company from one of its employees.

I ignored these signals. I couldn't ignore the final signal. That Friday I was asked to sit at the head table for a promotional lunch with a group of chief executive officers from our local business community. I was seated next to the CEO of this company. We were introduced, he asked about my work, and I told him about a job I was doing in team building for a leading software company. He became most enthusiastic. 'This is just what we need. Please come and talk with me on Monday.'

Had I been missing the signs? What did it teach me? It reminded me to keep an open mind to *coincidences* and be aware of them. To be aware peripherally and to prospect for business or ideas by using 'all round' vision. It reminded me that there are opportunities all around me and that I need to be aware of them and acknowledge them. I mean, really, what more could that company have done to get my attention!

4. Use pendulum thinking

Pendulum thinking is the ability to be able to see both sides of the argument and feel empathy with both. To be able to look at the adulterer and the person who she or he has been unfaithful to, and feel compassion for both. To be able to see the process the adulterer may have been through to do what they did, the pain, the suffering, the loneliness. To be able to feel empathy for them in their act of deception, and to be able to feel the pain that led them to that act.

It also means seeing the pain of the person they have been unfaithful to, of being wrongly done by, to understand the guilt of feeling it is their fault, the deception, the doubt, all of it. And to be able to feel empathy for them as well.

Pendulum thinking is to be able to watch the extremes of a situation and to be able to swing into the middle to feel the pain of both sides and to be able to feel, equally, compassion for both. It sounds tricky, and it certainly is not a natural state. However, pendulum thinking gives you the ability to understand the complete equation, opening your creativity to its maximum.

The second assault on the same problem
should come from a totally different direction.

TOM HIRSHFIELD

5. Great teachers are great learners

It is very hard to learn from someone who knows everything but is not prepared to share that knowledge freely and generously. It is like they have 'been there, done that, bought the T-shirt'.

It is the teachers at school or university who have a passion for their subject and are still learning about it that make the best and most interesting teachers. We had a biology teacher at high school. He was just out of teachers college. I can still see his face now, his eyes flashing, his words sometimes getting jumbled up because of his rush to get them all out. Mr Hacker was so enthusiastic, so happy to share his knowledge that he was always taking us out on field trips, always showing us how animals worked, how they were composed, how they were built, and how it all interrelated.

Mr Hacker stood out because of his passion for learning. It was never hidden, as with the English teacher, who would always show us how much she knew, how smart she was, but would never impart it to us because she could not add the magic ingredient, enthusiasm, to the message. The information she presented to us always seemed a little out of reach, as if she and the information were elite and we were not quite good enough to share it. Presented by her, her subject felt unattainable. It was too smart, too clever for us to absorb, so we never quite got it. We studied and got through our exams, but it was Mr Hacker from whom I learnt the most.

Apart from anything else, he taught me that in order to be a great teacher one also needs to be a great learner. Great learners make the best teachers because of their enthusiasm and their passion, their fun, their vulnerability, their joy in learning and their pleasure in giving and receiving.

Creative thinkers have the courage to be great teachers and great learners at the same time, because they know that this is the way to access the greatest knowledge.

Giving and receiving are the same.

IAN MATHIESON

6. *Break your limitations regularly*

Get out of your comfort zone, do something crazy, outside of your square. I was at a concert with a friend, a conservative but lovely man. We were at Shirley MacLaine's cabaret act. She was in fine form, dancing and singing with total exuberance. It was 1989 and at that time Shirley was getting a lot of abrasive press about her 'way out' ideas expressed in her 'spiritual' books. Everyone was expecting her to refer to her spiritual ideas during the cabaret, and you could tell that the audience was a little disappointed when she didn't share any of them. Just as she was coming to the end of the last bracket, she told us a story.

She was travelling to Peru, on one of her spiritual journeys. She disembarked from her flight and the people who were going to meet her were nowhere to be found. However, there was an old Peruvian man who was patiently waiting in a quiet corner of the airport. He approached her, offering her a ride. She accepted; she didn't know why she accepted, because he didn't tell her where his destination was.

Still, she felt that she must go, so she trusted this old man and they started a long dusty ride up into the Peruvian mountains. As night fell, the road became more narrow, more steep. As they drove up the mountain, the oxygen became thinner and she stopped asking questions. It was pointless anyway, because he would not answer her questions, he just drove.

Eventually, tired and cold, they arrived at the end of the road. The road seemed to go nowhere except for a cave off to one side. The old man took her over to the cave and told her to go inside, that she would find the meaning of life in there.

Enthusiasm rushed back into every fibre of her body. She soldiered on. On through the dark corners of the cave, deeper and deeper into an unknown space. She turned a corner and there was another old man, even older and wiser looking than the first.

He said, 'Child, come closer. What is your question?' Gleefully, Shirley answered, 'Could you please tell me the meaning of life?' Just at that moment this old man's face broke into the most wondrous smile and he burst out singing, 'Life is just a bowl of cherries'. And at that point the superb Shirley

MacLaine commenced singing this great little song, which she sang right the way to the end.

She had led us along, all the way, and we loved it. Every minute.

After her song, she talked about being outrageous, about breaking the rules and your limitations. She said, 'When you leave here tonight, within the next 24 hours, do something outrageous, something outside your comfort zone. Don't hurt anyone in the process, just break your barriers'.

Well, I left the show wondering how I could break my barriers, and was still thinking about it when my friend came over the next night, very excited about something. He bided his time. He waited until after dinner, and when he had everyone's attention he dropped his trousers and showed us his newly acquired tattoo. This 40 something, conservative businessman had broken his barriers. Of course, it was not visible to the general public, it was tucked away on his hip. But for him it was an outrageous act. No wonder I married him. Crazy man.

7. *Use visualisation as a tool*

The soul never thinks without a picture. Whatever you can visualise or see in your imagination you can achieve. In creative thinking, visualisation plays an enormous part. Once you have created the vision, dreamt the dream, you need to believe without the evidence. To do this you need to visualise the end result daily.

See the idea coming into fruition. See the end result, the achievement or goal, as if you have already achieved it. Gillette could not get financing for his razor blades for six years. Experts insisted it was not possible to put an edge on sheet steel that would shave. But Gillette knew that it could be done and kept a vision of that goal in his mind constantly.

Eventually he was able to help others to see it too. Gillette is now as synonymous to shaving as McDonalds is to hamburgers. Do you think we would be so familiar with the name Gillette today, without this man's ability to hold the vision, no matter what opposition he met with along the way?

Trust your subconscious mind, it has the answer. If it does not come immediately, turn it over to your subconscious while you sleep. On waking, watch for the signs. Guidance will come, but not necessarily from the direction you thought it would.

8. Believe in miracles

Right now there are miracles happening all around you. They may be miracles that you expect or they may be too tiny to warrant your attention. The interesting thing about miracles is that if you don't take the time to notice small miracles, when a big one comes your way, you may not notice it either.

Our culture has been so left brain, so analytical, so logical, that we have become cynical about miracles, or have relegated them to religious experiences outside our personal experience. Not so. Miracles are any occurrences that take you by surprise. Anything where you are given more than you expected or dreamt of is a miracle, any act of kindness is a miracle.

A close friend, Janis, had all her jewellery stolen, every piece. She felt enormous grief and sadness. She had strong, sentimental feelings about so many of the pieces: some were very old family heirlooms, some her husband had given her a long time ago. And on the day that the robbers came, she had left her wedding and engagement rings beside her bed. She had been rubbing hand cream onto her hands and forgotten to slip them back on.

She grieved for weeks and weeks, seeing her diamond engagement ring and wedding ring being stolen as symbolic of the tormented stage at which her marriage was at the time. Maybe, she thought, this was an omen that her marriage was also over.

Janis sat on the veranda one day and closed her eyes. She thought of all the love she felt for her husband, Steven. She thought of all the fun and joy she had with him over the years. She could see how hard and sad his face had become and, like a bolt of lightning, she saw the real symbolism of what the stolen jewellery was all about.

It was an opportunity to let go of the past and create a new beginning. As she sat and focused on this thought, a weight lifted from her shoulders. She felt light, she felt free, she felt love again. She felt love for herself, in having become so bogged down in the hardness and heaviness of the relationship. And she felt love for Steven, compassion for his fear and the feelings that led him to distance himself from her. She felt hope, she felt that now she had a chance, a chance to make a new beginning and create a new and purposeful start with their love. She felt that the past relationship was not working any more, that it had become invalid, and that she could create a new one, based on the same strong love but with renewed vigour.

When Steven walked into the house that night, he could feel the change, he could see it in her eyes. She was so excited about her discovery and the prospect of a renewed future for them both that the excitement and hope passed onto him. He began to feel it too.

That night they planned for their new future together. They were like young newly-weds, even though they were both in their fifties. At midnight, they decided to celebrate a new year. They opened a bottle of champagne that they had been saving for something special like a christening or a wedding, and they celebrated their new beginning. Their new future.

Years later, when they reflected back on the robbery, they saw this as a miracle. The miracle that had brought them back together again. It became a miracle for them. But another miracle also happened that night. As they were going to bed, they decided to move the bed closer to the window so they could hold each other and watch the stars as they drifted off to sleep. Under the footing of the bed were her rings. Both occurrences were miracles. Which miracle was the most miraculous? I know how Janis and Steven feel.

9. Be outrageous

Being outrageous will mean different things to different people. An outrageous act for some could be an everyday occurrence for others.

Beth didn't look the outrageous type. She had lived a full life, but felt there was something missing. She was an outrageous woman for her time. She had had many lovers; had travelled throughout the world; had been to every country in the world, and lived for a time in each.

At 78 years of age she was reviewing the life she had led as a young adult. She tried to remember what it was like to make love for the first time. Her mind went back to the place, the time, the face, and she tried to remember the feeling of love. She said she couldn't remember. She couldn't actually remember what it was like to make love, that first special time, but she could remember every act of kindness from that lover and from every lover who had been kind, every gentle word.

So when she looked back on her life, it wasn't about what she thought it was. The importance of life wasn't about having many conquests. It wasn't about living in all those countries. For her, it became about compassion, love, care and kindness. She realised that she hadn't lived such an outrageous life after all. She saw that the could have been more outrageous with her kindness, more indiscriminate with her kindness, could have been more childlike about her kindness. At the end of the day, for her, these things were what she remembered most and they became what she decided to do with the rest of her life.

A group of aged-care nurses told me that, in their experiences, the elderly are concerned about dying alone, in pain, and dying without forgiving, without finishing saying something or doing something to heal a relationship or friendship. Use your creative mind to do everything you feel you need to do. Don't let any stone go unturned. Have the courage to live your life with passion, with courage and with your creative thinking in top gear.

> *The best portion of a good person's life –*
> *their little nameless, unremembered*
> *acts of kindness and of love*

WILLIAM WORDSWORTH

I was working on a speech I had to give for a creative thinking workshop on the Gold Coast. I decided to challenge the group with a mental exercise.

I would ask each person to think of his or her favourite animal. The exercise was for the individual to take on the characteristics of that animal, the characteristics they admired. I would ask them to do this for one week, and see if this gave them more insight about using different qualities to see different things. I decided to try the exercise for a week myself first before asking the group to participate. I chose the sea eagle.

We live on the river in Brisbane, and opposite the place where we live is an island hugging the other side of the river bank. On this island there are two very big old trees, and in one of these trees is a great big nest. Here, perched high in the air, live two of the most beautiful, regal sea eagles I have ever seen. With wings outstretched, they glide effortlessly through the air. I watch them and always feel uplifted, better, more joyous after viewing their majestic gliding.

For me, the sea eagle represents grace, dignity, harmony, style and strength. The sea eagle flies above everything, gracefully surveying the beauty around it. I decided to add these qualities, and more, to my life in everything I did. I woke the first day and imagined how the sea eagle would rise, then looked at my day the way I thought the sea eagle would survey the day.

I was going along very well. I got into my car, ruffled my feathers and stuck my sharp beak out, noticing how much my posture improved when I adapted to this pose. I was going into the city to a special meeting with a client. As I was driving along the river road surveying the beauty all around me, I suddenly thought, 'Oh, no, I didn't bring my briefcase with the agenda and my notes.' I had forgotten to put it into the car, I was so busy thinking about the sea eagle.

I was almost there. It was too late to go back now. I had a flash of fear. I hate being seen as unprepared. Then I started to laugh, I mean really laugh. How ridiculous I was being; what would a sea eagle be doing with a briefcase anyway? Sea eagles don't need briefcases! And, of course, I didn't; I did fine without it.

The following are the highlights of the ideas I presented on creative thinking for this seminar.

Sea eagles don't need briefcases

WING COMMANDS:

Self motivation – contribute at a gut level

◆

Clear positive self talk – clean it up

◆

Catch people doing things right – and tell them

◆

Fix the problem – not the blame

◆

Create an environment for change

◆

Give yourself a 'whack' on the side of the head regularly

◆

Use creative visualisation as your magic wand

Being outrageous for me was to go to that meeting without the notes. It was also being a sea eagle for a week. It is different things to different people. You will know what is outrageous for you.

Break down your barriers

Be outrageous!
People who achieve mastery have
the ability to be outrageous.

GITA BELLIN

Creative Thinking

- ☑ Humour is creative thinking at work
- ☑ Identifying left and right brain thinking
- ☑ Intuition and creativity go hand in hand
- ☑ Recognise opportunity
- ☑ Move freely from right to left brain, then back
  to right again
- ☑ Expect a miracle
- ☑ Challenge the rules
- ☑ Trust your dreams
- ☑ Develop 'all round' vision
- ☑ Use pendulum thinking
- ☑ Great teachers are great learners
- ☑ Break your limitations regularly
- ☑ Use visualisation as a tool
- ☑ Believe in miracles
- ☑ Be outrageous
- ☑ Sea eagles don't need briefcases
- ☑ Break down your barriers

Creating Abundance

Getting What You Want

THE VEHICLE

Giving Yourself the Best

Elizabeth's story

Elizabeth felt pretty pleased with herself; she was happy, well, and full of life and energy, but there was one area of her life that she couldn't seem to get together. She was always a little short of money. At the end of the month after she had paid all her bills, she would be overdrawn in her cheque account.

She couldn't understand it; she had lots of money coming in, her business was going well. Lizzie's Home Made Food Company was working fine. The service she provided was of value; she enjoyed it and felt that her customers were getting great value for money. So why did she have this nagging problem with money all the time?

She would work it all out, down to the last dollar, then something would come up that would throw her calculations out completely. She felt she had paid her dues, that she had this part of her life under control, but she didn't. She thought about her attitude to money and decided to watch how she spent it for one month.

What she experienced when she made herself aware of it surprised her. She noticed how every time she paid a bill, she resented it, whether it were the rates on her home, or the supplies for her catering business. She noticed that she was not comfortable about paying out money and yet she was happy to be paid for her services and really enjoyed receiving payment from her customers.

All of a sudden, it hit her. She was 'out of exchange' about money. Happy to receive it but not happy to give it out. The cycle was incomplete. She realised that money was an energy to be used for exchange and she was resenting the exchange.

Elizabeth decided two things. To pay her bills with enthusiasm and pleasure, and to pay them on time. She

also sent out *thank you* notes to her suppliers with her cheques to let them know she appreciated their service and their products.

It turned her life around.

Her suppliers were delighted with her gesture and gave her the best products and best service. Her relationship with her suppliers improved and, most delightfully, her relationship with money changed. She started to enjoy the flow of it and saw it as a process rather than an event. Elizabeth's business and life became abundant.

Elizabeth's story

*Create as much wealth
as your heart desires.*

DEEPAK CHOPRA

Giving Yourself the Best

Giving yourself the best is a strong desire in most people, but is not always achievable. Often this is because you do not have the map, or the understanding, of how to go about it. Creating abundance is often seen as creating wealth, and although that's part of creating abundance, it is only a part of it. To truly create abundance, it is necessary to create it throughout your life. Create an abundance of pleasure, of joy, of laughter, of recognition of yourself and others. Create abundance in friendships, in opportunities, in growth, in ideas, in results, in nature and in love.

Work out your purpose in life

The first step in creating the abundance you desire is to work out your purpose in life. At least once in your lifetime, you may come to the point where you wonder if you are doing what you were destined to do. You can waste a lifetime waiting for the *right* thing to come along, the right job, person or career. This can stop you from making any movement or decision at all.

Be active, create a purpose in life, something to aim for, a focus. I was speaking with a friend, Margaret, recently. She was having a lot of difficulty with her focus. As a mother, wife, businesswoman, friend, she had lots of things to focus on. She decided to crystallise her thinking; she thought, 'If I were to die tomorrow, what would I like to have contributed to this wonderful place?' The answer didn't come easily, she was torn in all directions. As an environmentalist, she wanted to clean up the world. As a feminist, she wanted to create a wonderful environment in which to bring up her sons. As a businessperson, she wanted to succeed in her field.

After a deal of soul searching, she decided her purpose was to *bring love* to whatever endeavour she was doing. She was delighted with her choice, as she could apply it to every direction in her life.

Life is not anything, it is the opportunity for something

Your purpose may be world peace, it may be to make a million, it may be to become a powerful influence in the management of the nation or the local football club, or it may be simply to be happy. There is no best purpose. Whatever you come up with is perfect for you. But having a purpose contributes to your ability to create abundance, because then you have something that abundance can flow toward.

Create a belief system of abundance

The next important step in creating abundance is to create a belief system or philosophy of abundance, to believe that it is possible to have rather than not have, that there is plenty to go around. There is already an abundance available; it may just not be flowing toward you at the moment.

Deepak Chopra, a master at creating abundance, and his teacher Maharishi Mahesh Yogi were discussing a world peace project. Somebody asked, 'Where is all the money going to come from?', and he replied without hesitation, 'From wherever it is at the moment.'

So this is an important step, actually to believe that there is not only enough to go around, but plenty; all you have to do is attract it toward your purpose. And having a purpose to start off with is an essential part of this process. Once you have this purpose, you will need to believe without the evidence, to trust that you will be able to create what you need. You do this by setting goals for yourself, by working toward these daily and matching your behaviour to these goals.

Life is about learning, not perfection

Abundance is not about perfection. Because your life is designed for new experiences through learning, perfection is not possible. Perfection is about standing still, whereas having abundance is about movement which creates opportunities for growth and change. You are constantly presented with situations to embrace that are just beyond your present capacity, and these make the vehicle for you to create abundance and joy.

You can choose either to reject the flow of experiences or lessons and remain stuck in the *status quo* or to let go, to have a go and experience the joy of expanding. If you choose to regard life as a continual process of growth, you will add infinite meaning and direction to it.

Overwhelming events can be opportunities for change and for the unfolding of new strength and love within yourself. Failure may seem to be negative; however, it's a splendid chance for learning. Turning failure into success is a matter of one's state of mind. Success starts with commitment. Everything flows from that, so turn the failures around by setting goals that match your purpose and commitment.

Check that your intention is clear

Others will help you to create abundance throughout your life, especially if you look for the good intention behind unkind behaviour. Everything and everyone is on your side if you choose to see it that way. Have the courage to look for good when others are trying to organise, manipulate or upset you.

My friend Janet has just won an international award for leadership. She has been chosen by the owner of her worldwide personnel company as one of the world's four outstanding leaders in her field. Janet believes that it is not what you say, it is how you say it. It is how you treat your people that makes them work successfully as a team. She has this uncanny ability to look for the good in others. She always has something positive to say about her people. Some may call this naïve; I don't. I've watched her moving around a room talking to everyone as she goes. I've watched as she brings joy and pleasure to each person she talks to.

Her philosophy is to look for the strengths in others and to notice them. This clear insight into others' strengths gives her abundance in her relationships. Give yourself a chance to allow Janet's sort of clear insight to come into your relationships.

Follow your truth

If following the truth requires upsetting or dislodging others, then take courage, because you in fact help others around you the most if you speak your passion and your truth. If you have the courage to speak for what you desire and need most, you create an environment for love and achievement and abundance.

My daughter Cassie was being tutored by a very talented teacher, but came to me in a quandary. What she was being taught was not having any direct application to her schoolwork, and in her second last year at high school it needed to. Cassie was hesitant about telling Ellie, the tutor, because she liked her and liked working with her and she didn't want to upset their relationship. I said to Cassie, 'Darling, what are your choices?'

This is how she saw it. She could ring her up and make excuses about her sessions and not go. She could go and be unhappy, or she could tell Ellie how she felt and what she needed. When Cassie realised that her first two choices would actually do more harm to the relationship, she saw telling the truth as her only option.

Speaking up, with the chance of rejecting someone, is always a risk, but I believe that when you do speak up, you have the opportunity to heal a relationship. It may hurt initially but, if it is your truth at the time, eventually it will heal the relationship.

Trust yourself – you are your best teacher

Sometimes trusting yourself may mean a parting of the ways from some old thought pattern, a belief system or value system you have that doesn't serve you any more. It could be leaving a friend behind who you just can't be around any more because of their lack of understanding, or their fears.

This is how it happened for John. He had been a first grade footballer, and had played well for his country. He took over his father's business when he was thirty-five. It was a successful, medium-sized family business with 20 staff. In the boom time of the early 1980s John decided to expand. He decided to set up branches all over the country. In order to do this, he needed more people to help him, so he drew on his network of rugby friends to staff his branches.

One of his best mates on the football field was to set up the branch in Tasmania. The budget was set, everything was in place, the market was there for the product, and Bill was his mate, so he was confident that everything would go well with the branch.

But when things did not go well, John did not heed the warning signs. He would not take the advice of his accounting people to close down the branch. He said it just needed more time and everything would turn around. John's national sales manager talked to him every day about the figures. He even went down to the branch and discovered that Bill just wasn't putting the hours or commitment into the business. Still John would not listen.

It was only when the Tasmanian branch started to draw on the profits of the other successful branches that John became alarmed. The figures showed that if this were to continue, he would not have a business at all in six months time. Bill had to be told. The branch had to be closed down to protect the rest of the business.

It was one of the toughest things he had ever had to do. He went through hell finding a way to tell Bill about his decision. He had let his idea of friendship stand in the way of good judgement and he had paid the price. It was now time to let go, lick his wounds, and move on. A big part of creating abundance is the ability to be able to let go of something that doesn't work for you any longer and move on.

Friends are a great reflection of yourself

〜〜〜

Friends are a great reflection of yourself. In John's case, Bill reflected an area of his life that he was not prepared to look at, but that he couldn't afford not to look at. Friends can be wonderful mirrors. Cherish them and their lessons; they have great wisdom to impart – not necessarily the kind you may wish to hear or experience, but great wisdom just the same.

Doug and Jodie were best friends before they were married, which is why it was so tough for Jodie when Doug left her for another woman. They had been married for 15 years and had been friends for 10 years before that. Jodie's best friend, Adel, was sick of hearing her anger and tired of hearing her friend's whining. She knew it was time for Jodie to move on, time to go back out into the world and live life again. Adel was at the end of her rope. She had tried every way she could to bring her friend back to life. Finally she said:

> Jodie, it has been a year now and you have a different job than the one you had when you were with Doug, one that gives you more freedom. You wouldn't have taken that job if you had still been with him. You are back playing netball again, another thing you wouldn't have done if he was your partner. You live in a house that you love, one that he provided for you, and you still want to punish him for leaving you. You are still asking for unreasonable amounts of money from him. How big a price do you think he should pay for assisting you with your personal empowerment?

Jodie got it; it hit her like a ton of bricks. Yes, she had changed. Her life was more centred around the things she liked to do. She did have her life more like she wanted it as a result of his leaving her. It was time to move on.

Adel was a perfect mirror. She showed Jodie the truth, uncomfortable though it may have been. She gave her the opportunity to leave the past behind and get on with her new life.

The *mirrors* or reflections that irritate you the most can have the biggest impact. Do you have a friend whom you are enormously drawn to, but who also says and does things that drive you crazy?

Watch what drives you nuts. The things you don't like in others are often a reflection of the things you do not like in yourself. The qualities that person is displaying can be the qualities you least like to admit you have yourself. Look at everybody as being a person that can teach you something. Thinking 'What has this person come to teach me?' can give you much more insight into what is really happening in the situation. You draw your friends into your life for learning. Don't miss any lessons.

Be non-judgemental

Try not to be judgemental while learning the lessons, because attacking and criticising your friends won't create the learning experience. Being judgemental of others is a form of denial about yourself that will hold you back. You are denying the learning experience if you are overly judgemental. Listen for the real message in the communication process, be aware of what you are really learning; learn it and you probably won't be upset by that person any more.

Enemies teach us how to love

Value your enemies, or the people whom you dislike, just as much as your friends. Your enemies are also grand teachers. Listen to these people. Listen to the emotions, feelings, fears and thoughts these people bring up in you, as they are opportunities to learn about yourself. Enemies make just as valid reflections of yourself as friends.

When you need a friend, take an enemy to lunch. With only a slight adjustment, these can become your greatest friends. Remember, something drew you together in the first place.

Create a balanced lifestyle

Giving yourself an abundance of quality time is often the last thing on your list of things to do, and is not a natural state in this busy life we lead. But whether you are a student, a mother, a world leader, a professional sportsperson or a busy person on the go, it's an essential component for balance.

In creating abundance in your lifestyle, remember to create it for yourself too. It's so easy to get caught up in the *doing* of things and forget to give yourself some *customer service*. A great friend of mine, Patrick Maroney, when speaking about our friendship, said that sometimes we get caught up in the *doing* of things and don't put enough into friendships or relationships.

Try this process. Decide on 10 activities you like to do, activities that would give you particular pleasure, nourish you and help you to feel renewed and replenished. You may come up with 10 different activities, as I have here, or you may like a certain activity so much you wish to repeat it every day.

1 HOUR Singing/ piano lesson	**1 HOUR** Bush walking	**1 HOUR** Sitting in nature

1 HOUR One-on-one with each child a week (walking/talking outside of normal family stuff)	**1 HOUR – 90 MINS** Movie/video or film

1 HOUR Lunch with friends	**1 HOUR** Reading fiction or magazines	**1 HOUR** Visiting special friends

1 HOUR Massage	**1 HOUR** Learning a new game (E.g. mah-jong class)

Allocate an hour a day, early morning, lunchtime, afternoon or evening, to enjoy one of these activities. If you use a diary, schedule one each day at the beginning of the week. If you don't have a diary, get one or use a wall calendar. If a one hour session daunts you, then try half an hour and build on that. A woman I met in a country town recently told me that thinking about allocating an hour a day made her more stressed. She started with three half-hour sessions a week, and thought she was achieving tremendously with that. Rightly so; for her, that was a huge step in caring for her needs.

Use drawings or symbols to represent this valuable time, and draw them in your diary or on your wall planner. This time needs to be respected as if it were as important as an appointment with a valued client or friend. Reschedule when you have to, but respect this time – it is creating the personal abundance you need to rejuvenate your spirit.

Terry was a workaholic; he saw his value as being tied to his work. He was at this desk by 8.00 am and was never home till 7.30 or 8.00 pm at night. He gave little time to his family and no time at all to himself. He was horrified when I suggested he give some time to himself. He rejected the idea out of hand, saying he had no time for what he had to do, let alone anything else. I suggested that if he took the time out to replenish himself, he could be more effective and creative with the time he did have at work.

He decided to wake up an hour early each morning to do this and also decided to allocate an hour a day for his family as well. Terry is now reaping the benefits. He was running out of time because he was chasing it, rather than feeling the abundance of it by giving himself a more balanced lifestyle.

Create the flow of money

Having an attitude of abundance toward money is fundamentally believing there will be enough: enough for you, your needs, your desires and your wants. This attitude of enough has the most profound effect on your relationship with money. Think about this: there are children not even born yet who will amass vast amounts of money in their lifetime. In the United States alone, $2000 million changes hands daily. So there is abundance. Right now, more money is being made in the mint. So there is enough, there is plenty to go around. All you need to do is attract it to your ideas, projects or life.

Look at money as an energy like any other energy – like love, fear, hate or joy. It works as a part of the law of nature. Whatever you put in, you get out. View it in it's overall perspective. Money is always exchanged for good ideas, good value, good service. Exchange your qualities for money in the market-place and that will create your lifestyle. If you want to improve your lifestyle, then upgrade your qualities, your value. By upgrading your skills, education or knowledge, you can ask more for these skills in the marketplace.

That's the deal, and it's a fair one. I've seen people fold their arms and say I'll do more when I'm paid more. But it doesn't work that way. To create abundance, you need to show your intention to contribute more and that is shown by doing more than you are paid to do.

A public servant, Jean, told me recently that she always worked as if she was at the *next level*. That way she was always the one taking more responsibility for tasks and projects and always the one seen as doing more. Jean creates her own rise to the *next level* and the one after, and the one after that, by her attitude to her work and her attitude of giving more.

Give yourself quality

Give yourself quality. Make yourself feel special by giving yourself the best. Have fewer rather than more, if it means giving yourself a high quality product. Carla Zampatti, a successful designer of clothes and businessperson, said, 'The quality will be remembered long after the price has been forgotten.' She's right. I have a jacket of hers that is 10 years old and still looks fantastic.

Quality sets up a feeling of worth, that you are worthy of the best, so you should enjoy it. Deepak Chopra says, 'Go first class all the way.' Why? Because like attracts like. If you create an abundance of quality around you, you have set up the ground rules. Your intention is clear – you want the best, and that's what you will attract. Go without, rather than not give yourself the best.

Pay your bills with a big *thank you*. Accept responsibility for your bills, don't begrudge paying them. If you begrudge them, you are stopping the flow of money. Always write a note on the account when you pay it, or a thank you with the bill, to show the person from whom you have bought something that you value what has been exchanged. People who begrudge paying bills, like Charles Dickens' character, Scrooge, rarely enjoy true value.

Value your money as an energy, to give you your lifestyle, not something that's to be piled up in a vault and kept. The value of money is in its effective use and the flow of it, not in the hoarding of it. Rarely do you find a happy hoarder of money. I've met very *money*-wealthy people for whom it wouldn't matter how much they amassed, it would never be enough. It never seems to satisfy them and they have to have more.

Using money as an effective tool is an attitude of mind. It flows, so enjoy the process of that flow, don't begrudge it, or people who have it. Acknowledge the money-rich people in a positive way. Don't envy them. That's giving away your power to create it for yourself.

Congratulate the wealthy

When you see others achieving, congratulate them either outwardly (encouraging words or statements) or inwardly, to yourself (by saying, 'Good on them'). This acknowledges the abundant flow they have created. The more you honour the process, the more you will draw wealth to yourself.

We have created the 'tall poppy' syndrome in Australia, the politics of envy: those without condemning those with. Does it help those without to gain more? No, it has the opposite effect. Be pleased about the success of others. It doesn't mean there is less for you. We have already established there is plenty to go around.

In the 1970s there was an economic philosophy about competition whereby you needed to fight viciously for your slice of the market because the pie (the market) was only so big. People would see a pie as being the customer's need for a certain product and that there were only so many slices to go around. It was a very limiting way of seeing the marketplace, until a creative genius came along and said, 'Why can't we create a bigger pie!' In fact, that's just what happened.

If you have a great product that is priced well, then you can always make the pie bigger, you can always find a market for it. Every day the world shows us new inventions along the old themes. Create a bigger pie and expand the marketplace.

A healthy attitude about money will always create abundance. Make sure you are always *in exchange*, that what you buy and what you pay for is about equal, and be happy about that exchange. Enjoy it. Say 'thank you' with enthusiasm. Always remember to thank the person paying you for their payment of service or product. Enjoy the process, it will create more of the same.

Create your energy level

We all have an aura of energy around us. This is a subtle, surrounding glow, an atmosphere which surrounds every living thing. This aura is changing minute by minute, changing colour and changing in density. There are special cameras that can capture this on film.

How you nurture the level of your energy will have an enormous impact on this aura, and on your ability to create abundance in your life. Sitting quietly in nature and breathing deeply can raise your level of energy, bringing it back to its full strength again. You have the most impact on the level of your energy, through what you do, what you think, and how you feel. Nourish yourself, care for yourself, look after yourself. That does not stop you from caring for others; it means that you will be in a stronger position to serve or help others if you do have that high level of energy to work from.

Abundance visualisation exercise

Calm yourself, relax, close your eyes. Imagine you are in an enormous castle. This is a beautiful, splendid castle with huge turrets, lush gardens and a huge maze cut out from hedges.

There are hundreds of rooms in the castle, and you start your exploration from the ground floor. As you walk through the heavy wooden double doors, you notice to the right of the hall a big hearth with a large welcoming fire, blazing brightly. You stand in front of the fire and feel the abundance of warmth coming to you, filling your body with the heat you desire.

You decide to explore the rooms in the castle; you have the freedom to choose any door to walk through. You begin. The first door you open is the dining room. As you enter, you notice the large banquet table in the centre of the room; it is laden with an abundance of food and drink. The table is almost groaning with all your favourite foods. The table is laden with everything you have ever desired or enjoyed.

There is a large dining table near the window. At it are seated the nine most interesting people, past and present, you could imagine dining with in the whole world. They are all there. See them enjoying each other's company and eagerly waiting for you to join them. See their smiling, welcoming faces.

As you join them, the feast begins. Helpers come as if from nowhere and serve you all the things you love to eat. Watch all of your guests enjoy the food, the wine, the ambience, the friendship, the laughter and the joy.

Relax for a moment and create your scene as you would like it to be, as vividly as you can. Savour the moments, enjoy the experience.

When you are ready, and have enjoyed the food and the friendship, leave the table, walk out the door and climb the stairs. At the top of the stairs is a doorway. The doors are gilt, with carvings of fairies and angels etched in gold around the outside. You open the door. The room is full of your favourite flowers; everywhere there are large vases of the flowers you enjoy the most, in your favourite colours.

As you look past the flowers, you see that this is a grand bedroom, with a large king-size bed over near the balcony. It is a huge, four-poster bed with beautiful carvings inlaid with gold around the four posts.

You see your perfect partner waiting for you on the balcony. If you don't have a partner, imagine your dream person. In as much detail as possible, see your perfect partner waiting lovingly and patiently for you on the balcony. As you go to meet this loving person, notice the welcoming smile, the welcoming arms and the feeling of wholeness as you accept their love and warmth.

Now choose to go into whatever room you desire. Each room has the abundance you desire, of whatever you want. Decide to create another doorway and enjoy the room full of whatever abundance you wish.

When you feel you have been filled with your heart's desire, open your eyes and take the memory of the abundance you experienced with you as a reminder of what is possible and a reminder that there will always be enough for you.

Create wellness

You have probably heard the saying 'If you haven't got your health, then nothing else matters.' It is true. If you are feeling sick, it is extremely hard to enjoy a full and abundant lifestyle. That is why you need to create abundance in health and wellness, so you can enjoy what you have created.

Wellness begins with a healthy state of mind; everything flows from this. Having a good self image and self esteem creates a body abundant in wellness. Your self talk, the on-going conversation you have with yourself from birth to death, feeds your self image and esteem the most. The quality of your conversation determines the quality of your self image, which in turn feeds your mind, which in turn feeds the messages that go out to your body about how you feel. People who say things to themselves like 'I always get three colds every winter' ... 'I always get sick on holidays' ... 'I always get headaches in the afternoon' are usually right!

We program our self image through our self talk, very effectively. You may not have a choice about what people say to you, but you always have a choice about how you speak to yourself and others. Be aware of what you say to yourself; your self talk needs to be reassuring and supportive towards yourself about 80–90 per cent of the time if you desire to have a healthy body. You also need to be aware of the way you talk to others; this affects your health as well. Speak as you wish to be spoken to; this is the golden rule.

Taylor was unsettled with his life when we spoke last year. He seemed to be on the edge. He was fast becoming a workaholic and did not appear to be getting a lot of joy from his lifestyle. We talked about things he could do to be calmer and more balanced and discussed positive self talk as a means of calming his mind. He told me the most erratic time of the day for him was in the mornings when he arrived at work. On questioning him in more detail, we discovered the cause.

Taylor was a 'commentary driver'. Every morning as he drove to work, he spoke out loud giving an on-going commentary about what the other drivers were doing on the road, and it wasn't good. He was criticising their driving, their actions and yelling at them as he was driving along, using bad language and abusive words.

I explained to him how this works on the subconscious mind. As the subconscious has no moral or other judgement, it absorbs whatever you give it. In yelling and abusing others, his subconscious was absorbing the abuse as feedback. The subconscious cannot decipher the target; it heard and was absorbing it as self talk. Taylor's stress levels, his ability to start the day with an open mind, and his attitude were being affected by the wrong information. The subconscious mind responded to these abusive statements as if they were directed to him.

Once he realised the negative effect his abusive feedback was having upon his productivity and stress levels, he stopped, and re-programmed his thoughts. Instead of admonishing fellow drivers about their driving, he came to focus on his own safe and careful driving. The effect was miraculous. He began arriving to work happy and ready to go. Taylor re-chose his self talk and re-chose his feeling of wellness.

Having a balanced intake of food is a commitment to wellness. This list shows the balance you need to attract an abundance of health and wellness in your life.

◆ **EAT MOST**
  Bread (preferably choose wholegrain)
  Cereals, rice and pasta (preferably choose wholegrain)
  Legumes (dried peas, beans and lentils)
  Fruit
  Vegetables
  Water

◆ **EAT MODERATELY**
  Meat (preferably lean)
  Poultry (preferably without skin)
  Fish and seafood
  Eggs
  Milk, cheese (preferably choose low-fat or
    fat-reduced varieties)
  Nuts and seeds

◆ **EAT LEAST**
  Margarine, oil (preferably polyunsaturated or
    mono-saturated)
  Fat-reduced spreads
  Fatty foods
  Salt and salty foods
  Sugar and sugary foods
  Alcohol

Your fluid intake influences your health a great deal. Drinking plenty of water is wonderful for the body. Alcohol and caffeine (in coffee and in soft drinks) dehydrate the body, so it is important to increase the amount of water you drink when you are drinking alcohol and caffeine. You need 6 to 8 glasses of water a day for your body to feel the abundance it deserves to feel.

There are lots of schools of thought about exercise. There are those who say you must do more, those who say less. You must settle on the pattern that suits your body the most. Some choose a half-hour walk a day, some walk for an hour three times a week. My parents do 20 minutes of T'ai Chi every morning, and that suits their bodies very well. It is possible to keep fit with short bursts (say 10 minutes) of exercise three times a day. Ben, who has a job on the fifth floor of a city office building, always takes the stairs, and sees that as his fitness program. Jenny, who works on a production line, always takes a brisk walk outside in the company's grounds, rather than go on *smoko*, and she is happy to call that her fitness program.

To have abundant good health, you need a balance of fitness, even if it is to do stretching exercises when you wake in the morning. If you have ever watched a cat or dog after taking a long nap, they stretch every which way to satisfy their bodies. We should have the sense of a cat! Taking responsibility for your wellness is about seeing your weak areas and strengthening them, having the belief that you can influence your health by doing the preventative things mentioned here.

I don't believe that we are walking time bombs just waiting to go off, that sickness can strike whenever it wishes, that we are victims of any illness or virus that comes along. I believe you can maximise your wellness by taking responsibility for whatever you are feeling. Look for the real reason you are feeling ill or out of sorts. Look for the emotional key that may have triggered feeling ill. Then decide how you want to feel. It may take time, but we do have much more influence over our health than we will ever know.

Louise Hay in her book *You Can Heal Your Life* gives many choices for viewing your health and provides possible solutions for healing. She helps identify the cause by looking at the metaphysical reason for the unwellness, then gives a possible solution and a positive affirmation for you to say to start turning that problem around. This process has been a particularly successful process in our family for the last 10 years. We always look for possible emotional reasons for the imbalance (and sickness is just an imbalance), take responsibility for having created it on some level and set about healing it through affirmations, diet, massage, talking about it, creating action and nurturing ourselves while we are getting better.

As a precious child, you were always cared for when you were sick – put to bed, given lots of pampering and love. Thankfully this happens for children, but many people grow up seeing this as the only way they have of gaining attention. As a nine-year-old child, I gave Mum and Dad a lot of concern and worry by being sick nearly every week, creating a tantrum every time and not wanting to go to school. What I couldn't admit then, but believe now, was that it was my way of getting the love and attention I felt I needed at the time. I wasn't getting it at school and I wanted to stay home and get it from my mother.

Luckily for my parents, I grew out of it. But some never do. They see the love and sympathy that they get when they are sick as supporting their value. It is not.

Your value is in just being you. We need to stop rewarding people for getting sick by way of only giving them love and concern at that time. Our value to ourselves is when we are strong and well and we need to reward ourselves and each other for being well, through showing love, care and concern all the time, not just when we are sick.

Sonya was attending a talk I gave recently and tried this on her family when she went home. Instead of only asking for attention when she was sick, she propped herself up in bed, with her favourite bedclothes on, having prepared her special tea, set the TV up so she could see it, and put her favourite books out to read.

When her husband came home, she said, 'Darling, I'm not going to get sick to gain the attention I need at the moment. Please pamper me tonight. Please treat me like you treat me when I am sick, as I need nurturing tonight, and I'm never again going to get sick to get the nurturing.' She was asking for what she wanted in her relationship and breaking a life time of habit by rewarding herself for being well, rather than being sick.

Access critical mass

Critical mass is an important ingredient in creating abundance. Critical mass is when enough attention is given to an idea or project for that idea or project to achieve a momentum of its own, catapulting it toward the desired result. It's when enough people believe something and then it occurs. The fall of the Berlin Wall is an example of critical mass. Enough people rested their finger on the Berlin Wall and it came tumbling down. The worldwide desire was for this to happen and enough people put their attention to it and it happened. Because of the electronic press, it has become even easier to create critical mass about a whole range of global issues.

Creating critical mass can be done through enlisting others around you to share your vision or goal, working towards it yourself, showing your intent and putting your attention on it every day. When an idea has enough support or interest, it then becomes self propelling, and you have created critical mass. Keep trying, keep persisting, keep talking about your dream. Create your own abundance through using critical mass to achieve your dreams.

Never, Never, Never give up.

WINSTON CHURCHILL

Create Happiness

By creating happiness and fun in the workplace and in their home environment, everyone can accomplish so much more. By banishing fear and insecurity within your team, whether at home or work, you create a more abundant environment, an environment that is more productive and pleasant. You will find people around you doing the things they love and loving more about the things they do.

Try laughing more in your home and in your workplace. An environment that has laughter is infinitely more productive. Create a mindset that allows laughter in as well as out. Look for the opportunity to be funny and light, rather than being serious and heavy all the time.

Create a new direction

You may have many desires, new directions, new stirrings and new passions. All of these are what you desire at the time – there is never an ultimate. It's the journey, it's the learning, not the destination, that is important. The journey is the prize, and as soon as you reach that understanding, that prize, another will beckon you from out of the corner of your eye. Be totally in the moment, whatever that moment is. The point of power is in the present. This is not a rehearsal for life. This is it! Speak your truth as quickly as possible and, hopefully, you will never grow up.

Life in abundance comes through having passion

Learn your lessons quickly and move on.

EILEEN CADDY

239

Creating Abundance

- ☑ Work out your purpose in life
- ☑ Life is not anything, it is the opportunity for something
- ☑ Create a belief system of abundance
- ☑ Life is about learning, not perfection
- ☑ Check that your intention is clear
- ☑ Follow your truth
- ☑ Trust yourself – you are your best teacher
- ☑ Friends are a great reflection of yourself
- ☑ Be non-judgemental
- ☑ Enemies teach us how to love
- ☑ Create a balanced lifestyle
- ☑ Create the flow of money
- ☑ Give yourself quality
- ☑ Congratulate the wealthy
- ☑ Create your energy level
- ☑ Create wellness
- ☑ Access critical mass
- ☑ Create happiness
- ☑ Create a new direction
- ☑ Life in abundance comes through having passion

Further Reading

Here are some valuable books for further reading:

Bach, Richard, *Illusions*, Pan Books, 1977.

Bach, Richard, *The Bridge Across Forever* (a love story), William Morrow & Co. Ltd., USA, 1984.

Bennett, Vicki, *Mirrors – An Adventure into Ourselves*, Boolarong Publications, Brisbane, 1992.

Bennett, Vicki, *Take Me To My Garden, Mummy*, Sunshine Publications Pty Ltd, Brisbane, December, 1985.

Blanchard, Kenneth & Spencer, Johnson, *The One Minute Manager*, William Morrow & Co. Ltd., USA, 1981.

Bolton, Robert, *People Skills*, Simon & Schuster Australia, Sydney, 1987.

Chopra, Deepak, *Ageless Body, Timeless Mind*, Harmony Books (division of Crown Publishers, Inc.), New York, 1993.

Chopra, Deepak, *Creating Affluence*, New World Library, California, 1993.

Cohen, Alan, *The Dragon Doesn't Live Here Anymore*, Alan Cohen Publications, Somerset, N.J., 1981.

Cohen, Herb, *You Can Negotiate Anything*, Lyle Stuart Inc., Seraucus, N.J., 1980.

Cole-Whittaker, Terry, *What You Think of Me is None of My Business*, The Berkley Publishing Group, New York, 1979.

Covey, Stephen R., *Principle-Centered Leadership*, Simon & Schuster Inc., New York, 1990.

Covey, Stephen R., *The Seven Habits of Highly Effective People*, Information Australia, Melbourne, 1990.

Edwards, Betty, *Drawing on the Right Side of the Brain*, J.P. Tarcher Inc., USA, 1979.

Fulghum, Robert, *All I Really Need to Know I Learned in Kindergarten*, Grafton Books, Great Britain, 1989.

Gawain, Shakti, *Creative Visualisation*, New World Library, California, 1978.

Green, Barry with Gallwey, W. Timothy, *The Inner Game of Music*, Doubleday & Company, Inc., New York, 1986.

Gray, John, *Men Are From Mars, Women Are From Venus*, Harper Collins Publishers Inc., Sydney, 1992.

Harris, Thomas A., *I'm OK—You're OK*, Jonathan Cape Ltd (as *The Book of Choices*), Great Britain, 1970.

Harrison, Dr John, *Love Your Disease*, Angus & Robertson Publishers, Sydney, 1984.

Hay, Louise L., *Heal Your Body*, Specialist Publications, Sydney, 1986.

Hayward, Susan, *A Guide for the Advanced Soul*, In-Tune Books, Sydney, 1985.

Kouzes, James M. & Posner, Barry Z., *The Leadership Challenge*, Jossey-Bass Inc., Publishers, San Francisco, 1987.

Linn, Denise, *Pocketful of Dreams*, A Triple Five Publication (a division of Nacson & Sons Pty. Ltd.), Sydney, 1988.

Lynch, Dudley & Kordis, Paul L., *Strategy of the Dolphin*, Ballantine Books, New York, 1988.

Maltz, Maxwell, *Psycho-Cybernetics*, Simon & Schuster Inc., New York, 1960.

Millman, Dan, *Way of the Peaceful Warrior—A Book that changes Lives*, H.J. Kramer, Inc., California, 1984.

Oech, Roger Von, *A Whack on the Side of the Head*, Warner Books Inc., UK, 1990.

Peck, M. Scott, *The Road Less Travelled* (first and second editions), Simon & Schuster Inc., New York, 1978.

Redfield, James, *The Celestine Prophecy*, Transworld Publishers (Aust) Pty Ltd., Sydney, 1994.

Redfield, James & Adrienne, Carol, *An Experiential Guide*, Warner Books Inc., New York, 1995.

Rico, Gabriele Lusser, *Writing the Natural Way*, J.P. Tarcher, Inc., Los Angeles, 1983.

Rose, Colin, *Accelerated Learning*, Accelerated Learning Systems Ltd., Aylesbury, Bucks, Great Britain, 1985.

Sher, Barbara with Smith, Barbara, *I Could Do Anything, If Only I Knew What It Was*, Hodder Headline Australia Pty Ltd., Sydney, 1995.

Silva, José, *The Silva Mind Control Method* (For Business Managers), Prentice-Hall Inc., Englewood Cliffs, N.J., 1983.

Silva, José, *The Silva Mind Control Method*, Souvenir Press Ltd., Great Britain, 1978.

Sweetland, Ben, *Grow Rich While You Sleep*, Prentice-Hall, Inc., USA, 1962.

Sweetland, Ben, *I Can*, Cadillac Publishing Co., Inc., New York, 1953.

Waitley, Denis, *The Psychology of Winning*, Nightingale-Conant Corporation, Chicago, 1993.

Ziglar, Zig, *See You at the To*p, Pelican Publishing Company Inc., Louisiana, 1974.

About Vicki Bennett

I have been training people in the corporate and government sectors since 1970. This can mean I have learnt a lot or I am still learning. I believe that I am learning more now than ever.

The business sector is going through a quickening, a period of time where people choose to learn quickly and access global critical mass. This accelerates change and growth both globally and individually.

MY VISION IS:

> *To be of service and to contribute to the marketplace by being a valuable catalyst for change and growth.*

So that I can contribute to the quickening as a valuable resource, I teach personal empowerment. I believe that if we empower ourselves and each other, we can maximise the opportunities around us. This means taking risks, challenging the old rules, contributing more and being responsible for our relevance through continued learning.

Vicki Bennett Training has worked with many large corporations in the areas of integrity based customer service and team building. In recent years we have worked with many companies, including Mobil Oil Australia Pty Ltd, empowering their dealers and their teams to provide integrity based customer service to the marketplace. We have also recently worked in the aged care sector, empowering caregivers with skills and attitudes to give this same integrity based customer service to residents in nursing homes.

Vicki Bennett Training is contributing to raising the benchmark of customer service in Australia and believes that we can all contribute to giving this excellence in customer service by giving more in the marketplace, more effective customer service to ourselves, our family, our community, our teams and our consumer. Vicki Bennett Training has been contributing to this since 1980.